MONTE CARL

Make it Fresh

Front cover: Blueberry Crumble Pie, page 87; photography by Colleen Duffley, styling by Brooke Leonard.

Editor: **Alyson Moreland Haynes**

Graphic Designer: **Amy Heise**

Managing Editor: **Kay Fuston**

Production Manager: **Liz Rhoades**

Assistant Food Editor: **Joe Watts**

Staff Writer: **Kate Neale Cooper**

Copy Editor: **Carol Boker**

Copy Intern: **Jennifer Wegman**

Food Intern: **Niccole Davis**

Photographers: **Ralph Anderson, Jim Bathie, Tina Cornett, Colleen Duffley, Becky Luigart-Stayner, Randy Mayor, Howard L. Puckett**

Photo Stylists: **Cindy Manning Barr, Kay E. Clarke, Virginia R. Cravens, Connie Formby, Trinda Gage, Mary Lyn Hill Brooke Leonard, Cathy Muir, Fonda Shaia, Ashley J. Wyatt**

Weight Watchers Magazine Test Kitchen Director: **Kathleen Phillips**

Editor, *Weight Watchers* Magazine: **Kate Greer**

Executive Editor: **Melissa Chessher Aspell**

Art Director: **Austin Davis**

Editorial Coordinator: **Christine O'Connell**

Senior Vice President, Publisher: **Jeffrey C. Ward**

General Manager: **Thomas C. Marshall**

Business Manager: **Michael W. Stern**

Marketing Manager: **Betsey Hummel**

Production Manager: **Brent Kizzire**

Assistant Production Manager: **Carolyn Dewberry Cooper**

President and CEO: **Tom Angelillo**

Executive Vice President: **Bruce Akin**

Executive Vice President: **Scott Sheppard**

Vice President, Administration: **Jeanetta Keller**

Vice President, Consumer Marketing: **Hallett Johnson III**

Vice President, Circulation: **Pat Vander Meer**

Vice President, Magazine Production: **Larry Rinehart**

Vice President, Finance: **Bruce Larson**

Back cover: Sesame-Crusted Chicken With Pineapple Salsa, page 9; photography by Colleen Duffley, styling by Brooke Leonard.

WELCOME

Fresh is a word that reinvents itself as we go through life. Kind of like "love." Remember how you defined love as a 16-year-old? Heaven forbid you should be held to that definition—homecoming mums, late-night phone-a-thons, and all—for a lifetime. And just as "love" means one thing to one person and something entirely different to another, the definition of fresh varies depending on whom you ask. To your grandmother, a fresh meal was one made from scratch. But as we near the end of the twentieth century, we appreciate the fact that picking the meal off the vine yourself isn't always practical. Today "fresh" conveys many things: Sometimes it's a few canned goods that make a soup a snap or a store-bought angel food cake that shaves precious time off the recipe for Raspberry Angel Torte. But "fresh" always conveys the time and effort you put into making a meal for family and friends.

Of course, we're not talking about a lot of time and effort. *Make It Fresh: More Than 150 Recipes for a Healthy You* is grounded in two beliefs: First, meals should be a healthy balance between minimal time and maximum taste and nutrition; and second, the best foods are those in which wholesomeness is evident in every spoonful. In line with that thinking, we've created recipes that use shortcuts, simple ingredients, and sometimes even convenience products to make homemade doable for you. There's a shrimp-and-couscous salad that can be made the day before you serve it, a focaccia bread made with frozen dough, and a sophisticatedly simple dessert that requires a mere three ingredients (Strawberries With Balsamic Vinegar). Of course, it's important to remember that using canned fruits or frozen vegetables doesn't mean you compromise nutrition. Vegetables and fruit are packaged within hours of harvesting, when they're at their nutritional peak. So they deliver as many nutrients as the stuff you have to squeeze and sniff in the produce section.

To let you know where you stand nutritionally, each recipe in this cookbook includes *POINTS,* the basis for following the new Weight Watchers 1•2•3 Success™ Weight Loss Plan. We've also counted all the calories—along with the fat, protein, carbohydrates, fiber, cholesterol, iron, sodium, and calcium—and included diabetic exchanges for people with special dietary restrictions. So whether you're trying to make good use of all that fruit from the u-pick farm or putting together a quick weeknight meal, you'll find recipes on these pages that fit your definition of fresh.

Alyson M. Haynes

Make it Fresh

c o n t e n t s

Main Dishes

REVITALIZE YOUR SPIRIT WITH THE
GOODNESS OF A HOME-COOKED MEAL.

**Sesame-Crusted Chicken
With Pineapple Salsa**

Italian Sausage With
Peppers and Onions

Sesame-Crusted Chicken With Pineapple Salsa

In the 20 minutes that the chicken bakes, there's time to make and chill this easy salsa.

½ cup sesame seeds
2 tablespoons peeled minced fresh ginger
2 teaspoons vegetable oil
½ teaspoon salt
4 (4-ounce) skinned, boned chicken breast
   halves
Cooking spray
Pineapple Salsa

1. Preheat oven to 350°.

2. Spread sesame seeds in a shallow baking pan; bake at 350° for 5 minutes or until toasted, stirring after 2½ minutes. Let cool. Increase oven temperature to 400°.

3. Combine sesame seeds, ginger, oil, and salt in a small bowl; stir well. Spread mixture evenly over chicken, and place on a broiler pan coated with cooking spray.

4. Bake at 400° for 20 minutes or until tender. Serve with Pineapple Salsa. Yield: 4 servings (serving size: 1 breast half and 6 tablespoons salsa).

POINTS: 7; **Exchanges:** 1 Fruit, 4 Very Lean Meat, 3 Fat
Per serving: CAL 330 (41% from fat); PRO 29.5g; FAT 15.1g (sat 2.3g); CARB 18.8g; FIB 1.9g; CHOL 72mg; IRON 4mg; SOD 364mg; CALC 200mg

Pineapple Salsa:

1 (15¼-ounce) can pineapple tidbits,
   drained
½ cup chopped red bell pepper
¼ cup chopped fresh cilantro
1 tablespoon fresh lime juice
1 teaspoon peeled grated fresh ginger
¼ teaspoon hot sauce
Dash of ground cloves

1. Combine all ingredients in a medium bowl; stir well. Cover and chill 15 minutes. Yield: 1½ cups.

Italian Sausage With Peppers and Onions

Olive oil-flavored cooking spray
¾ pound turkey Italian sausage, cut into
   ¾-inch-thick slices
2 cups sliced onion

1 cup green bell pepper strips
1 cup yellow bell pepper strips
1 cup fat-free, no-salt-added spaghetti sauce
1 (8-ounce) can no-salt-added tomato sauce
½ cup water
1 teaspoon dried Italian seasoning
4 garlic cloves, minced
6 (1-inch-thick) slices French bread,
   toasted
Hot sauce (optional)

1. Coat a large nonstick skillet with cooking spray; place over medium heat until hot. Add sausage, onion, and bell peppers; sauté 10 minutes. Add spaghetti sauce and next 4 ingredients; bring to a boil. Reduce heat; simmer, uncovered, 10 minutes. Spoon sausage mixture evenly over bread slices. Sprinkle with hot sauce, if desired. Yield: 6 servings.

POINTS: 5; **Exchanges:** 1 Hi-fat Meat, 2 Starch, 1 Veg
Per serving: CAL 269 (22% from fat); PRO 13.5g; FAT 6.7g (sat 2.8g); CARB 38.2g; FIB 2.9g; CHOL 32mg; IRON 2.6mg; SOD 841mg; CALC 46mg

Hamburger-Mushroom Pizza

1 (16-ounce) loaf unsliced Italian bread
½ cup traditional-flavored bottled pizza
   sauce
8 (⅛-inch-thick) slices onion, separated into
   rings
1 cup presliced mushrooms
6 ounces ultra-lean ground beef
1 teaspoon dried Italian seasoning
½ teaspoon garlic powder
¼ teaspoon crushed red pepper
1½ cups (6 ounces) shredded pizza double-
   cheese (a blend of part-skim mozzarella
   and cheddar cheese)

1. Preheat oven to 500°.

2. Cut bread loaf in half horizontally. Place both halves of bread, cut side up, on a large baking sheet. Spread ¼ cup pizza sauce over each half of bread. Divide onion rings and mushrooms evenly between bread halves. Crumble beef into ½-inch pieces, and divide beef evenly between bread halves. Sprinkle Italian seasoning, garlic powder, and red pepper evenly over each pizza, and top each with ¾ cup cheese.

3. Bake at 500° for 9 minutes or until beef is done and cheese melts. Cut each half into 3 equal pieces. Yield: 6 servings (serving size: 1 piece).

POINTS: 6; **Exchanges:** 2½ Starch, 1½ Med-fat Meat
Per serving: CAL 301 (29% from fat); PRO 15.1g; FAT 9.7g (sat 2.7g); CARB 35.4g; FIB 2g; CHOL 31mg; IRON 2mg; SOD 542mg; CALC 155mg

Corned Beef-Cabbage Pizza

1   (10-ounce) can refrigerated pizza crust dough
Cooking spray
2   ounces thinly sliced lean deli corned beef
1   (10-ounce) bag angel hair slaw
¼   teaspoon salt
⅛   teaspoon pepper
¾   cup fat-free traditional pasta sauce
½   cup (2 ounces) finely shredded part-skim mozzarella
¼   cup grated Parmesan cheese

1. Preheat oven to 425°.

2. Unroll dough; pat dough into bottom and ½ inch up sides of a 13- x 9-inch baking dish coated with cooking spray. Bake at 425° for 7 minutes or until crust begins to brown. Remove from oven; set aside.

3. Cut corned beef crosswise into thin strips, and set aside.

4. Coat a large nonstick skillet with cooking spray; place over medium heat until hot. Add slaw, salt, and pepper; sauté 7 minutes or until wilted. Set aside.

5. Spread sauce over pizza crust, and spread slaw mixture over sauce. Top with corned beef, and sprinkle with cheeses. Bake at 425° for 14 minutes or until crust is golden. Serve immediately. Yield: 4 servings.

POINTS: 7; **Exchanges:** 2½ Starch, 1 Veg, 1 Fat, ½ Hi-fat Meat
Per serving: CAL 323 (25% from fat); PRO 11.7g; FAT 8.8g (sat 3.3g); CARB 43.2g; FIB 1.7g; CHOL 26mg; IRON 0.8mg; SOD 1,082mg; CALC 195mg

Sausage-and-Egg Casserole

1   pound bulk turkey breakfast sausage
3   cups (½-inch) cubed white bread (about 6 slices)
2   cups skim milk

1½ cups egg substitute
½   cup (2 ounces) shredded reduced-fat sharp cheddar cheese
1   teaspoon dry mustard
Cooking spray

1. Preheat oven to 350°.

2. Cook sausage in a large nonstick skillet over medium-high heat until browned, stirring to crumble. Drain well.

3. Combine sausage and next 5 ingredients in a 13- x 9-inch baking dish coated with cooking spray; stir well. Bake at 350° for 45 minutes or until a wooden pick inserted in center comes out clean. Yield: 9 servings.

Note: Look for this sausage product in the fresh-meat or freezer section of the grocery store.

POINTS: 3; **Exchanges:** 1 Starch, 1½ Lean Meat
Per serving: CAL 157 (27% from fat); PRO 14.4g; FAT 4.7g (sat 1.7g); CARB 13.1g; FIB 0.4g; CHOL 23mg; IRON 1.2mg; SOD 471mg; CALC 150mg

Linguine With Spicy Beef and Artichokes

½   pound ground round
2   cups low-fat vegetable primavera spaghetti sauce
1   cup water
2   tablespoons tomato paste
½   teaspoon crushed red pepper
3   garlic cloves, crushed
1   (14-ounce) can quartered artichoke hearts, drained
5   cups hot cooked linguine (about 10 ounces uncooked pasta)

1. Cook meat in a large nonstick skillet over medium-high heat until browned, stirring to crumble. Drain well, and return to pan. Stir in spaghetti sauce, water, tomato paste, red pepper, and garlic. Bring to a boil; reduce heat, and simmer, uncovered, 10 minutes. Stir in artichoke hearts; cover and simmer 2 minutes. Serve over linguine. Yield: 5 servings (serving size: 1 cup pasta and 1 cup sauce).

POINTS: 7; **Exchanges:** 3½ Starch, 1 Veg, 1 Lean Meat
Per serving: CAL 345 (10% from fat); PRO 20.6g; FAT 3.8g (sat 1.1g); CARB 56.9g; FIB 1.7g; CHOL 28mg; IRON 4.5mg; SOD 505mg; CALC 65mg

Shrimp-and-Couscous Salad

For a ready-and-waiting summer supper, assemble this salad the night before.

4¼ cups water
1   lemon, sliced
1¼ pounds large shrimp
1½ cups cooked couscous
½   red bell pepper, chopped
1   (14-ounce) can artichoke hearts, drained and coarsely chopped
¼   cup light mayonnaise
⅓   cup fresh lemon juice
3   tablespoons chopped fresh dill
½   teaspoon pepper
¼   teaspoon salt

1. Combine water and lemon slices in a Dutch oven; bring to a boil. Add shrimp, and cook 3 minutes or until shrimp turn pink. Drain and rinse under cold water. Discard lemon. Peel shrimp, and cut in half lengthwise.

2. Combine shrimp, couscous, bell pepper, and artichoke hearts in a bowl; toss well. Combine mayonnaise and next 4 ingredients; stir well. Pour over shrimp mixture; toss well. Cover and chill at least 2 hours. Divide salad evenly among 4 individual plates. Yield: 4 servings.

POINTS: 5; **Exchanges:** 1½ Starch, 2 Very Lean Meat, 1 Fat
Per serving: CAL 234 (24% from fat); PRO 19g; FAT 6.2g (sat 1g); CARB 25.7g; FIB 0.7g; CHOL 113mg; IRON 2.7mg; SOD 367mg; CALC 41mg

Grilled Red Snapper With Pesto

1   cup fresh basil leaves
¼   cup parsley sprigs
¼   teaspoon salt
⅛   teaspoon pepper
1   small shallot, peeled and quartered
1   small garlic clove, peeled
1   tablespoon lemon juice
1   tablespoon olive oil
2   (8-ounce) red snapper fillets
Cooking spray
1   large tomato, cut into 8 wedges

1. Place first 6 ingredients in a food processor; process until finely chopped. With processor on, slowly pour lemon juice and olive oil through food chute; process until smooth. Place fillets in a shallow dish. Spread 1 tablespoon basil mixture

Lemon and dill add a fresh flavor to Shrimp-and-Couscous Salad.

Lamb-and-Spinach Pilaf

over both sides of fillets; cover and chill 30 minutes. Set aside remaining basil mixture.

2. Prepare grill. Arrange fillets in a wire grilling basket coated with cooking spray. Place basket on grill rack, and grill 4 minutes on each side or until fillets flake easily when tested with a fork. Cut each fillet in half, and place on individual plates. Top each with 1 tablespoon basil mixture and 2 tomato wedges. Yield: 4 servings.

POINTS: 4; **Exchanges:** 3 Very Lean Meat, 1 Fat, 1 Veg
Per serving: CAL 166 (29% from fat); PRO 24.2g; FAT 5.3g (sat 0.8g); CARB 4.9g; FIB 1.2g; CHOL 42mg; IRON 0.8mg; SOD 205mg; CALC 53mg

Lamb-and-Spinach Pilaf

2   cups no-salt-added beef broth
1   cup uncooked bulgur or cracked wheat
¼   teaspoon salt
1   pound lean ground lamb
1   cup chopped onion
½   cup raisins
½   cup water
2   tablespoons lemon juice
½   teaspoon ground cinnamon
¼   teaspoon salt
¼   teaspoon pepper
¼   teaspoon ground nutmeg
1   (10-ounce) bag fresh spinach, chopped

1. Bring broth to a boil in a medium saucepan; add bulgur and ¼ teaspoon salt. Cover, reduce heat, and simmer 15 minutes or until bulgur is tender and liquid is absorbed. Set aside; keep warm.

2. Cook lamb in a Dutch oven over medium heat until browned, stirring to crumble. Drain in a colander. Wipe pan drippings with a paper towel.

3. Return lamb to pan; add onion and next 7 ingredients. Bring to a boil; cover, reduce heat, and simmer 7 minutes. Add spinach; cover and simmer an additional 3 minutes or until spinach wilts.

4. Divide bulgur mixture evenly among 6 individual plates. Top each serving with ⅔ cup lamb mixture. Yield: 6 servings.

POINTS: 4; **Exchanges:** 2 Starch, 2 Lean Meat
Per serving: CAL 269 (20% from fat); PRO 22.1g; FAT 6.1g (sat 2.1g); CARB 32.7g; FIB 7.4g; CHOL 54mg; IRON 3.4mg; SOD 289mg; CALC 82mg

Turkey-Veggie Meatballs

For more moist, more flavorful meatballs, use ground turkey that contains light and dark meat rather than just breast meat.

1½ pounds ground turkey
½   cup dry breadcrumbs
½   cup (2 ounces) finely shredded fresh
     Parmesan cheese
⅓   cup finely chopped green onions
¼   cup shredded carrot
¼   cup shredded zucchini
¼   cup chopped fresh parsley
¼   teaspoon salt
¼   teaspoon pepper
1   large egg white
2   garlic cloves, crushed
Cooking spray

1. Preheat oven to 400°.

2. Combine first 11 ingredients in a bowl; stir well. Shape mixture into 30 (1½-inch) meatballs. Place on a broiler pan coated with cooking spray. Bake at 400° for 15 minutes or until done. Yield: 30 meatballs (serving size: 5 meatballs).

POINTS: 5; **Exchanges:** ½ Starch, 2 Very Lean Meat, 2 Lean Meat
Per serving: CAL 228 (29% from fat); PRO 30.3g; FAT 7.3g (sat 3.1g); CARB 8.5g; FIB 0.8g; CHOL 71mg; IRON 2.5mg; SOD 399mg; CALC 166mg

Apricot-Glazed Ham

1   (2-pound) lean, boned center-cut ham, cut
     into 8 slices
Cooking spray
⅓   cup apricot preserves
2   tablespoons orange juice
2   tablespoons spicy hot mustard
1   teaspoon low-sodium soy sauce
½   teaspoon peeled grated fresh ginger

1. Preheat oven to 325°.

2. Arrange ham slices in a 13- x 9-inch baking dish coated with cooking spray. Combine preserves and next 4 ingredients in a small bowl; stir well. Spoon mixture evenly over ham slices.

3. Cover and bake at 325° for 15 minutes or until thoroughly heated. Yield: 8 servings.

POINTS: 4; **Exchanges:** 3 Lean Meat, ½ Starch
Per serving: CAL 186 (28% from fat); PRO 22.3g; FAT 5.8g (sat 1.9g); CARB 10.4g; FIB 0.2g; CHOL 53mg; IRON 1mg; SOD 1,198mg; CALC 14mg

Veal Piccata

1   pound veal cutlets (about ¼ inch thick)
¼   cup all-purpose flour
Cooking spray
1   teaspoon olive oil
½   cup dry sherry
¼   cup fresh lemon juice
2   tablespoons capers
Lemon slices (optional)
Chopped fresh parsley (optional)

1. Dredge cutlets in flour. Coat a nonstick skillet with cooking spray. Add oil; place over medium-high heat until hot. Add cutlets; cook 3 minutes on each side. Place on a platter. Set aside; keep warm.

2. Add sherry, juice, and capers to skillet, scraping skillet to loosen browned bits. Cook over medium-high heat until reduced by half, stirring occasionally. Serve over cutlets. Garnish with lemon slices and fresh parsley, if desired. Yield: 4 servings.

POINTS: 4; **Exchanges:** ½ Starch, 3 Very Lean Meat, ½ Fat
Per serving: CAL 178 (24% from fat); PRO 24g; FAT 4.6g (sat 1.1g); CARB 8.7g; FIB 0.2g; CHOL 94mg; IRON 1.5mg; SOD 435mg; CALC 26mg

Molasses-Grilled Pork Tenderloin

This recipe is pictured on page 32.
4   (¾-pound) pork tenderloins
¼   cup molasses
2   tablespoons coarse-grained Dijon mustard
1   tablespoon cider vinegar
Cooking spray

1. Trim fat from tenderloins. Combine tenderloins, molasses, mustard, and vinegar in a zip-top plastic bag. Seal bag, and marinate in refrigerator 8 hours, turning bag occasionally.

2. Prepare grill. Remove tenderloins from bag; discard marinade. Insert a meat thermometer into thickest portion of 1 tenderloin. Place tenderloins on grill rack coated with cooking spray; cover and cook 20 minutes or until thermometer registers 150° (slightly pink), turning occasionally. Let stand 5 minutes before slicing. Yield: 12 servings (serving size: 3 ounces).

POINTS: 4; **Exchanges:** 3½ Very Lean Meat, ½ Starch
Per serving: CAL 169 (24% from fat); PRO 25.9g; FAT 4.5g (sat 1.5g); CARB 4.8g; FIB 0g; CHOL 83mg; IRON 1.7mg; SOD 87mg; CALC 24mg

Curried Pork Tenderloin

1 pound pork tenderloin
1 tablespoon brown sugar
2 teaspoons curry powder
1 teaspoon dry mustard
½ teaspoon salt
½ teaspoon Hungarian sweet paprika
½ teaspoon pepper
Cooking spray
½ cup mango chutney

1. Preheat oven to 425°.

2. Trim fat from tenderloin. Combine sugar and next 5 ingredients; stir well. Rub tenderloin with spice mixture.

3. Place tenderloin on a broiler pan coated with cooking spray. Insert a meat thermometer into thickest portion of tenderloin. Bake at 425° for 25 minutes or until thermometer registers 150° (slightly pink). Let stand 5 minutes before slicing. Serve with chutney. Yield: 4 servings (serving size: 3 ounces pork and 2 tablespoons chutney).

POINTS: 5; **Exchanges:** 1½ Starch, 3 Very Lean Meat
Per serving: CAL 240 (17% from fat); PRO 25.2g; FAT 4.6g (sat 1.4g); CARB 24.2g; FIB 0.5g; CHOL 79mg; IRON 2.2mg; SOD 420mg; CALC 28mg

Italian Meat Sauce

1½ pounds ground round
2 cups sliced mushrooms
½ cup chopped onion
2 large garlic cloves, minced
¼ cup dry red wine
2 teaspoons dried Italian seasoning
¼ teaspoon salt
¼ teaspoon black pepper
⅛ teaspoon ground red pepper
1 (28-ounce) can tomato purée

1. Crumble meat into a microwave-safe colander; set colander in a glass pie plate. Microwave at HIGH 8 minutes or until browned, stirring every 3 minutes; discard drippings. Set meat aside.

2. Combine mushrooms, onion, and garlic in a 3-quart casserole. Cover with wax paper, and microwave at HIGH 5 minutes or until onion is tender. Add meat, wine, and remaining ingredients to casserole; stir well. Cover and microwave at HIGH 6 minutes or until thoroughly heated, stirring after 3 minutes. Serve over pasta. Yield: 8 servings (serving size: ¾ cup).

POINTS: 3; **Exchanges:** 2 Lean Meat, 2 Veg
Per serving: CAL 176 (28% from fat); PRO 20.6g; FAT 5.4g (sat 2g); CARB 12.5g; FIB 2.8g; CHOL 53mg; IRON 2.9mg; SOD 512mg; CALC 34mg

Mussels and Shallot-Wine Sauce

48 small mussels (about 1¼ pounds), scrubbed and debearded
1 tablespoon cornmeal
4 cups rock salt
½ cup dry red wine

This robust Italian Meat Sauce will become a family favorite.

MICROWAVE MAGIC

Microwaves are part of our everyday lives. You can't beat one for small tasks such as warming leftovers, making popcorn, or melting margarine. But the microwave can do a lot more.

Vegetables cooked in the microwave retain most of their nutrients, crispness, and color because little, if any, water is needed. Microwaves are perfect for making sauces because you don't need to stir frequently and you spend less time cooking.

But use the wrong container and you may be left with a dinner that tastes like plastic or contains broken glass. To test whether a dish is microwave safe, place a 1-cup glass measure filled with water in the microwave along with the container. Heat at HIGH for 1 minute. If the dish remains cool, it's safe for microwaving. If it's slightly warm, it is probably safe for heating or reheating, but not for cooking. If the dish is hot, don't use it in the microwave.

½ cup red wine vinegar
1 tablespoon minced shallots
¼ teaspoon cracked pepper

1. Preheat oven to 500°.

2. Place mussels in a large bowl; cover with cold water. Sprinkle with cornmeal; let stand 30 minutes. Drain; rinse mussels.

3. Place rock salt in the bottom of a shallow roasting pan. Arrange mussels in a single layer on rock salt. Bake at 500° for 5 minutes or until shells open. Remove mussels from pan; set aside, and keep warm. Discard rock salt and any unopened shells.

4. Combine wine, vinegar, shallots, and pepper in a small saucepan. Place over medium heat, and cook 5 minutes or until thoroughly heated. Serve with mussels. Yield: 4 servings (serving size: 12 mussels and ¼ cup wine sauce).

POINTS: 2; **Exchanges:** ½ Starch, 2 Very Lean Meat
Per serving: CAL 108 (22% from fat); PRO 14g; FAT 2.6g (sat 0.5g); CARB 6.2g; FIB 0.1g; CHOL 33mg; IRON 4.1mg; SOD 217mg; CALC 23mg

Southwestern Turkey

Skinned, boned chicken breasts are a good substitute for turkey cutlets.

Cooking spray
1 pound (¼-inch-thick) turkey breast cutlets, cut into 2½- x ½-inch strips
1¼ teaspoons chili powder
¼ teaspoon ground cumin
1 teaspoon vegetable oil
1¼ cups green bell pepper strips
1 cup thinly sliced onion, separated into rings
1 cup frozen whole-kernel corn
¾ cup thick and chunky salsa

1. Coat a large nonstick skillet with cooking spray, and place over high heat until hot. Add turkey strips, and stir-fry 3 minutes. Stir in chili powder and cumin. Remove turkey from skillet, and set aside.

2. Heat oil in skillet over medium-high heat. Add bell pepper strips and onion; stir-fry 3 minutes. Return turkey to skillet. Add corn and salsa;

stir-fry 2 minutes or until thoroughly heated. Yield: 4 servings (serving size: 1 cup).

POINTS: 4; **Exchanges:** 1 Starch, 3½ Very Lean Meat
Per serving: CAL 211 (16% from fat); PRO 29.1g; FAT 3.8g (sat 0.9g); CARB 15.6g; FIB 3.5g; CHOL 68mg; IRON 2.2mg; SOD 372mg; CALC 37mg

Cranberry-Ginger Pork Chops

4 (6-ounce) lean center-cut loin pork chops
½ cup thawed cranberry juice cocktail concentrate
3 tablespoons sliced green onions
1 tablespoon peeled grated fresh ginger
¼ teaspoon ground red pepper
Cooking spray

1. Trim fat from chops. Combine chops, juice, and next 3 ingredients in a zip-top plastic bag. Seal bag, and marinate in refrigerator 8 hours, turning bag occasionally.

2. Remove chops from bag, reserving marinade.

3. Prepare grill. Place chops on a grill rack coated with cooking spray; grill 5 minutes on each side or until slightly pink (150°), basting frequently with reserved marinade. Yield: 4 servings.

POINTS: 8; **Exchanges:** 2½ Fruit, 3½ Lean Meat
Per serving: CAL 342 (30% from fat); PRO 24.4g; FAT 11.4g (sat 4.1g); CARB 34.7g; FIB 0.2g; CHOL 77mg; IRON 1.6mg; SOD 69mg; CALC 17mg

Marinated Venison Steaks

6 (4-ounce) lean, boned venison loin steaks (about ½ inch thick)
¼ cup dry red wine
1½ tablespoons low-sodium soy sauce
¾ teaspoon dried thyme
¼ teaspoon salt
¼ teaspoon pepper
¼ teaspoon hot sauce
1 garlic clove, minced
1 bay leaf
Cooking spray

1. Trim fat from steaks. Place steaks, wine, and next 7 ingredients in a zip-top plastic bag. Seal bag, and shake until marinade ingredients are blended. Marinate in refrigerator 8 hours, turning bag occasionally.

It's hard to believe our creamy Chicken à la King is low-fat.

2. Prepare grill. Remove steaks from bag, reserving marinade. Discard bay leaf. Place steaks on grill rack coated with cooking spray; grill 3 minutes on each side or until desired degree of doneness, basting occasionally with reserved marinade. Yield: 6 servings.

POINTS: 3; **Exchanges:** 3½ Very Lean Meat
Per serving: CAL 133 (19% from fat); PRO 24.8g; FAT 2.8g (sat 1g); CARB 0.4g; FIB 0.1g; CHOL 92mg; IRON 4.1mg; SOD 209mg; CALC 11mg

Chicken à la King

4   (1-ounce) slices whole-wheat bread, toasted
1   tablespoon reduced-calorie stick margarine
3   (4-ounce) skinned, boned chicken breast halves, cut into bite-size pieces
¼   cup chopped onion
¼   cup sliced mushrooms
¼   cup all-purpose flour
2   cups skim milk
¼   cup frozen green peas, thawed
1   (2-ounce) jar diced pimiento, drained
½   teaspoon salt
½   teaspoon pepper
¼   teaspoon paprika

1. Trim crusts from toast, and cut each slice into 4 triangles; set aside.
2. Melt margarine in a large nonstick skillet over medium heat. Add chicken and onion; sauté 4 minutes or until chicken is browned. Add mushrooms; sauté 1 minute. Stir in flour; cook 1 minute, stirring constantly. Gradually add milk, stirring constantly until blended. Add peas and next 3 ingredients; cook until thick, stirring constantly. Divide toast triangles evenly among 4 plates; top each serving evenly with chicken mixture. Sprinkle with paprika. Yield: 4 servings.

POINTS: 5; **Exchanges:** 1½ Starch, ½ Sk Milk, 2½ Very Lean Meat
Per serving: CAL 254 (14% from fat); PRO 28g; FAT 4g (sat 0.6g); CARB 26.4g; FIB 1.7g; CHOL 53mg; IRON 2.1mg; SOD 573mg; CALC 192mg

Simple Roasted Chicken

1   (5- to 6-pound) roasting chicken
Cooking spray

1   teaspoon dried herbs (such as basil,
    oregano, or thyme)
¼   teaspoon salt
⅛   teaspoon pepper

1. Preheat oven to 450°.

2. Remove giblets and neck from chicken; discard. Rinse chicken under cold water; pat dry. Trim excess fat.

3. Place chicken on a broiler pan coated with cooking spray. Insert meat thermometer into meaty part of thigh, making sure not to touch bone. Coat chicken with cooking spray; sprinkle with herbs, salt, and pepper.

4. Bake at 450° for 30 minutes. Reduce oven temperature to 400°; bake an additional 45 minutes or until thermometer registers 180°. Discard skin before serving. Yield: 8 servings (serving size: 3 ounces chicken).

POINTS: 4; **Exchanges:** 2 Lean Meat, 1½ Very Lean Meat
Per serving: CAL 163 (36% from fat); PRO 24.6g; FAT 6.4g (sat 1.7g); CARB 0.1g; FIB 0g; CHOL 76mg; IRON 1.1mg; SOD 146mg; CALC 19mg

Steamed Orange Roughy With Herbs

This unbelievably simple recipe uses fresh herbs to guarantee a flavorful, low-fat meal.

½   cup parsley sprigs
½   cup fresh chives
½   cup thyme sprigs
½   cup rosemary sprigs
2   (8-ounce) orange roughy fillets
Lemon slices

1. Arrange half of herbs in a steaming basket. Top with fillets and remaining herbs. Steam, covered, 7 minutes or until fish flakes easily when tested with a fork. Cut each fillet in half. Serve with lemon. Yield: 4 servings (serving size: 3 ounces).

Note: Any mild-flavored white fish can be substituted in this recipe. Try cod, grouper, snapper, or farm-raised catfish. Don't limit yourself to the herbs we suggest; use any fresh herb you have available.

POINTS: 2; **Exchanges:** 2½ Very Lean Meat
Per serving: CAL 79 (10% from fat); PRO 16.7g; FAT 0.8g (sat 0g); CARB 0g; FIB 0g; CHOL 23mg; IRON 0.2mg; SOD 72mg; CALC 15mg

Grilled Scallops With Black Beans

1   pound sea scallops
1   teaspoon olive oil
1   teaspoon ground cumin, divided
¼   teaspoon ground red pepper
Cooking spray
1   cup diced onion
2   large garlic cloves, minced
½   cup finely chopped red bell pepper
2   cups drained canned black beans
1   teaspoon balsamic vinegar

1. Place scallops in a shallow dish. Combine olive oil, ½ teaspoon cumin, and ground red pepper; drizzle over scallops, and toss gently. Cover and marinate in refrigerator 30 minutes, stirring occasionally.

2. Coat a large nonstick skillet with cooking spray; place over medium-high heat until hot. Add onion and garlic; sauté until tender. Add red bell pepper; sauté until tender. Stir in remaining ½ teaspoon cumin and black beans; sauté 3 minutes or until thoroughly heated. Remove from heat; stir in vinegar. Set aside, and keep warm.

3. Prepare grill. Remove scallops from dish, and thread onto 4 (8-inch) skewers. Place skewers on grill rack coated with cooking spray; grill 3 minutes on each side or until scallops are done. Spoon black bean mixture evenly onto individual serving plates. Arrange grilled scallops evenly over black bean mixture. Serve immediately. Yield: 4 servings.

POINTS: 5; **Exchanges:** 3 Very Lean Meat, 2 Starch
Per serving: CAL 266 (10% from fat); PRO 28.7g; FAT 3.1g (sat 0.4g); CARB 31.4g; FIB 5.3g; CHOL 37mg; IRON 3.2mg; SOD 460mg; CALC 72mg

Broiled Lamb Patties

Cooking spray
½   cup finely chopped onion
⅓   cup finely chopped celery
1   pound lean ground lamb
1   cup fresh breadcrumbs
2   teaspoons ketchup
1   teaspoon Worcestershire sauce
½   teaspoon dried Italian seasoning

Beef and Broccoli With
Sun-Dried Tomatoes

¼ teaspoon salt

¼ teaspoon pepper

1. Coat a small nonstick skillet with cooking spray, and place over medium heat until hot. Add onion and celery; sauté 5 minutes.

2. Combine onion mixture, lamb, and remaining ingredients in a large bowl; stir well. Divide mixture into 6 equal portions, shaping each into a 4-inch patty. Place patties on a broiler pan coated with cooking spray. Broil 4 minutes on each side or until desired degree of doneness. Yield: 6 servings.

POINTS: 4; **Exchanges:** ½ Starch, 2½ Lean Meat
Per serving: CAL 184 (36% from fat); PRO 22.2g; FAT 7.4g (sat 2.5g); CARB 6.1g; FIB 0.6g; CHOL 68mg; IRON 1.8mg; SOD 230mg; CALC 30mg

Beef and Broccoli With Sun-Dried Tomatoes

½ pound lean, boned top round steak

¾ ounce sun-dried tomatoes, packed without oil (about 10)

½ cup boiling water

Cooking spray

½ teaspoon vegetable oil

2 cups broccoli florets

¼ cup sliced green onions

1 garlic clove, minced

2 teaspoons cornstarch

6 tablespoons dry white wine

¼ cup low-sodium soy sauce

2 cups hot cooked long-grain rice

1. Trim fat from steak, and slice steak diagonally across grain into thin strips. Set aside.

2. Combine tomatoes and boiling water; let stand 5 minutes. Drain; thinly slice tomatoes, and set aside.

3. Coat a wok or large nonstick skillet with cooking spray; place over medium-high heat until hot. Add steak; stir-fry 2 minutes. Remove steak from wok; set aside, and keep warm. Add oil to wok; place over medium-high heat until hot. Add broccoli; stir-fry 3 minutes. Add tomatoes, green onions, and garlic; stir-fry 1 minute.

4. Combine cornstarch, wine, and soy sauce; stir well. Return steak to wok. Add cornstarch mixture; stir-fry 1 minute or until thick and bubbly. Serve over rice. Yield: 2 servings (serving size: 1 cup steak mixture and 1 cup rice).

POINTS: 9; **Exchanges:** 3½ Starch, 2 Veg, 3 Lean Meat
Per serving: CAL 473 (13% from fat); PRO 36.1g; FAT 6.9g (sat 2g); CARB 66.6g; FIB 4.1g; CHOL 65mg; IRON 5.9mg; SOD 1,278mg; CALC 100mg

Moroccan Lamb Chops

1 teaspoon ground cumin

1 teaspoon Hungarian sweet paprika

1 teaspoon ground coriander

Moroccan Lamb Chops are rubbed with an aromatic savory-sweet spice blend.

CHOP CHOP

Lamb chops are easy to prepare and take only a few minutes to cook. They generally taste best when cooked rare to medium—be careful not to overcook them. When you head to the market, you'll find a variety of chops. Here's a guide to what's available.

Rack of lamb, the cut called for here, comes from the rib section and can be cut into chops or presented whole. Like the rib eye of a beef steak, lamb rib chops are tender and flavorful, making them perfect for quick, high-heat cooking. For this recipe, ask your butcher to French-cut the rack, which leaves an eye of meat on each chop with a naked, elegant bone.

Loin chops, which look like mini T-bone steaks, are one of the more expensive cuts of lamb but also one of the most tender. They can often be used interchangeably with rib chops but can't be French-cut.

½ teaspoon salt
¼ teaspoon ground cloves
¼ teaspoon ground red pepper
2 (1½-pound) French-cut lean racks of lamb, 8 ribs each
Cooking spray
1 tablespoon currants (optional)
6 cups hot cooked couscous

1. Preheat oven to 425°.

2. Combine first 6 ingredients; stir well. Rub lamb with spice mixture; let stand 5 minutes.

3. Place racks of lamb on a broiler pan coated with cooking spray. Bake at 425° for 25 minutes or until desired degree of doneness. Let stand 10 minutes before slicing into chops.

4. Stir currants into cooked couscous, if desired. Serve chops over couscous. Yield: 8 servings (serving size: 2 rib chops and ¾ cup couscous).

POINTS: 6; **Exchanges:** 2 Lean Meat, 2 Starch
Per serving: CAL 279 (25% from fat); PRO 21.1g; FAT 7.9g (sat 2.7g); CARB 30.4g; FIB 1.6g; CHOL 52mg; IRON 2.9mg; SOD 200mg; CALC 18mg

Meatball Stroganoff

1 pound ground sirloin
½ cup fresh breadcrumbs
6 tablespoons skim milk
1 tablespoon reduced-calorie stick margarine, melted
1 teaspoon salt
2 teaspoons minced fresh onion
Dash of ground nutmeg
Dash of ground cloves
Dash of pepper
1 tablespoon reduced-calorie stick margarine
Cooking spray
2 tablespoons all-purpose flour
1 (14¼-ounce) can no-salt-added beef broth
½ cup fat-free sour cream

1. Combine first 9 ingredients in a bowl; stir well. Shape mixture into 24 (1-inch) balls.

2. Melt 1 tablespoon margarine in a large non-stick skillet coated with cooking spray over medium heat. Add meatballs; cook 8 minutes or until browned, turning frequently.

3. Remove meatballs from skillet; set aside, and keep warm. Wipe drippings from skillet with a paper towel. Place flour in skillet. Gradually add beef broth, stirring with a whisk until blended. Place over medium heat, and cook 3 minutes or until slightly thick, stirring constantly. Remove from heat; stir in sour cream. Return meatballs to skillet; cook over medium heat 3 minutes or until meatballs are thoroughly heated (do not boil or sour cream will curdle). Serve over rice or egg noodles. Yield: 4 servings (serving size: 6 meatballs and about ½ cup sauce).

POINTS: 6; **Exchanges:** ½ Starch, 4 Lean Meat
Per serving: CAL 258 (33% from fat); PRO 29.7g; FAT 9.4g (sat 2.9g); CARB 9.7g; FIB 0.2g; CHOL 76mg; IRON 3.2mg; SOD 775mg; CALC 48mg

Crustless Chicken-and-Broccoli Quiche

For the roasted chicken, you can use leftover chicken or purchase a roasted chicken from your supermarket deli.

2 cups coarsely chopped broccoli florets
Cooking spray
2 tablespoons dry breadcrumbs
3 tablespoons all-purpose flour
1 teaspoon dried basil
¼ teaspoon salt
⅛ teaspoon pepper
1 cup 1% low-fat milk
1 tablespoon Dijon mustard
1 (4-ounce) carton egg substitute
1½ cups chopped roasted chicken
½ cup (2 ounces) shredded reduced-fat extra-sharp cheddar cheese, divided
¼ teaspoon paprika

1. Preheat oven to 350°.

2. Cook broccoli in boiling water 3 minutes or until crisp-tender; drain.

3. Coat a 9-inch pie plate with cooking spray; sprinkle with breadcrumbs (do not remove excess breadcrumbs). Set aside.

4. Combine flour, basil, salt, and pepper in a large bowl. Add milk and mustard, stirring with a whisk until blended. Stir in egg substitute. Add chicken and ¼ cup cheese; stir well. Pour mixture

into prepared pie plate. Sprinkle with remaining ¼ cup cheese and paprika. Bake at 350° for 45 minutes or until set. Let cool on a wire rack 15 minutes. Yield: 6 servings.

POINTS: 3; **Exchanges**: 2 Very Lean Meat, ½ Med-Fat Meat, ½ Starch
Per serving: CAL 167 (29% from fat); PRO 18.7g; FAT 5.3g (sat 2.1g); CARB 10.9g; FIB 1.9g; CHOL 39mg; IRON 1.6mg; SOD 353mg; CALC 186mg

Chicken Tostadas

1   pound skinned, boned chicken breast halves, cut into ¾-inch cubes
½   cup fresh lime juice
4   (8-inch) flour tortillas
½   teaspoon salt
¼   teaspoon pepper
Cooking spray
1   cup picante sauce
2   tablespoons finely chopped fresh cilantro
2   tablespoons low-fat sour cream
4   cups thinly sliced lettuce
2   medium tomatoes, chopped
6   mushrooms, sliced

1. Preheat oven to 350°.

2. Combine chicken and lime juice in a zip-top plastic bag. Seal bag, and marinate in refrigerator 30 minutes.

3. Place tortillas on a baking sheet; bake at 350° for 4 minutes or until tortillas are lightly browned and crisp. Set aside.

4. Remove chicken from bag; discard lime juice. Sprinkle chicken with salt and pepper. Coat a large nonstick skillet with cooking spray; place over medium heat until hot. Add chicken; sauté 4 minutes or until done. Stir in picante sauce, cilantro, and sour cream; cook 5 minutes, stirring occasionally (do not boil).

5. Divide chicken mixture evenly among tortillas; top with lettuce, tomatoes, and mushrooms. Cut into wedges, and serve immediately. Yield: 4 servings.

POINTS: 6; **Exchanges**: 3 Very Lean Meat, 1½ Starch, 2 Veg, 1 Fat
Per serving: CAL 314 (18% from fat); PRO 32.1g; FAT 6.1g (sat 1.5g); CARB 32.4g; FIB 2.7g; CHOL 69mg; IRON 3.3mg; SOD 1,210mg; CALC 112mg

Serve Chicken Tostadas with Easy Spanish Rice, page 29.

Salads and Sides

THE BEST SIDE DISH IS MORE THAN ONE OF
THE EXTRAS; IT'S THE UNDERSTUDY THAT
JUST MIGHT STEAL THE SHOW.

Taj Tabbouleh

Taj Tabbouleh

There's a method to this fix-and-forget-it layered salad. The salt pulls water out of the vegetables—which, in turn, softens the bulgur as it chills overnight.

½ cup uncooked bulgur or cracked wheat
2 tablespoons fresh lemon juice
1½ tablespoons olive oil
½ cup finely chopped green onions
2 garlic cloves, minced
2 cups finely chopped tomato
1¼ cups finely chopped celery
¾ cup finely chopped fresh parsley
1 cup seeded finely chopped cucumber
½ teaspoon salt

1. Combine first 3 ingredients in a 2-quart bowl; stir well. Layer green onions, garlic, tomato, celery, parsley, and cucumber over bulgur mixture. Sprinkle salt over cucumber. Cover and chill 24 hours. Toss well before serving. Yield: 5 servings (serving size: 1 cup).

POINTS: 2; **Exchanges:** 1 Starch, 1 Veg, ½ Fat
Per serving: CAL 116 (36% from fat); PRO 3.2g; FAT 4.6g (sat 0.6g); CARB 17.9g; FIB 4.8g; CHOL 0mg; IRON 1.6mg; SOD 277mg; CALC 47mg

Basil-Wrapped Corn on the Cob

4 ears corn
2 teaspoons reduced-calorie stick margarine, melted
¼ teaspoon salt
¼ teaspoon freshly ground pepper
24 large fresh basil leaves

Enjoy the flavors of summer with Basil-Wrapped Corn on the Cob.

1. Preheat oven to 450°.

2. Remove husks and scrub silks from corn; set corn aside. Combine margarine, salt, and pepper in a bowl; stir well. Brush margarine mixture over corn. Place each ear on a piece of heavy-duty aluminum foil. Place 3 basil leaves under each ear of corn and 3 leaves on top of each ear. Wrap foil around each ear, twisting at ends to seal.

3. Place foil-wrapped corn on a baking sheet. Bake at 450° for 15 minutes or until tender. Yield: 4 servings.

Note: To grill, prepare corn as directed above. Prepare grill. Place corn on grill rack; grill 15 minutes or until tender, turning every 5 minutes.

POINTS: 2; **Exchanges:** 1½ Starch
Per serving: CAL 106 (20% from fat); PRO 3.1g; FAT 2.4g (sat 0.3g); CARB 22.1g; FIB 3.2g; CHOL 0mg; IRON 0.6mg; SOD 180mg; CALC 24mg

Fresh Fruit With Mint-Balsamic Tea

Serve this versatile compote on lettuce leaves as a salad to complement dinner or in a large bowl for a brunch.

1½ cups water
¼ cup sugar
1 regular-size tea bag
½ cup fresh mint sprigs
1 tablespoon balsamic vinegar
2 cups cubed fresh pineapple
1 cup cubed honeydew melon
1 cup cubed cantaloupe
1 cup orange sections
1 cup blueberries

1. Combine water and sugar in a heavy saucepan; bring to a boil. Add tea bag and mint. Remove from heat; let steep 5 minutes. Remove tea bag; stir in balsamic vinegar, and let stand 5 minutes.

2. Pour mixture through a fine sieve into a bowl; discard mint. Add fruit, stirring gently to coat. Cover and chill at least 1 hour. Yield: 5 servings (serving size: 1 cup).

POINTS: 2; **Exchanges:** 2 Fruit
Per serving: CAL 126 (4% from fat); PRO 1.2g; FAT 0.5g (sat 0.1g); CARB 32g; FIB 4.5g; CHOL 0mg; IRON 0.5mg; SOD 9mg; CALC 28mg

Fresh Fruit With
Mint-Balsamic Tea

If you love the classic Italian pie, try Mostaccioli Pizza Salad.

Elegant Cheesy Broccoli

1½ pounds broccoli
1   tablespoon cornstarch
¼   teaspoon paprika
1   cup skim milk
¾   cup (3 ounces) reduced-fat Havarti cheese

1. Trim off large leaves of broccoli, and remove tough ends of lower stalks. Cut broccoli into spears. Steam broccoli, covered, 10 minutes or until crisp-tender. Arrange broccoli on a serving dish; set aside, and keep warm.

2. Combine cornstarch and paprika in a saucepan; gradually add milk, stirring constantly with a whisk until blended. Place over medium heat; cook until thick, stirring constantly. Add cheese; cook until cheese melts, stirring constantly. Pour over broccoli. Serve immediately. Yield: 6 servings.

POINTS: 2; **Exchanges:** ½ Med-fat Meat, 2 Veg
Per serving: CAL 98 (40% from fat); PRO 7.9g; FAT 4.4g (sat 1.7g); CARB 8.5g; FIB 2.2g; CHOL 15mg; IRON 0.9mg; SOD 142mg; CALC 99mg

Mostaccioli Pizza Salad

3   tablespoons white vinegar
2   tablespoons water
1   tablespoon olive oil
¾   teaspoon dried Italian seasoning
¼   teaspoon salt
¼   teaspoon pepper
2   garlic cloves, crushed
2¾ cups cooked mostaccioli (about 1½ cups uncooked large tubular macaroni)
1   cup presliced mushrooms
¾   cup cherry tomatoes, halved
½   cup chopped green bell pepper
½   cup (2 ounces) shredded part-skim mozzarella cheese
Additional cherry tomatoes (optional)

1. Combine first 7 ingredients in a medium bowl, stirring with a whisk until blended. Add pasta and next 4 ingredients; toss gently to coat. Cover and chill. Garnish with additional cherry tomatoes, if desired. Yield: 5 servings (serving size: 1 cup).

POINTS: 4; **Exchanges:** 1½ Starch, 1 Fat
Per serving: CAL 164 (28% from fat); PRO 6.6g; FAT 5.2g (sat 1.6g); CARB 22.3g; FIB 0.8g; CHOL 7mg; IRON 0.8mg; SOD 174mg; CALC 86mg

Okra, Corn, and Tomatoes

4   ears corn
Cooking spray
1   medium onion, chopped
1   small green bell pepper, seeded and chopped
3   large tomatoes, peeled and chopped
1   teaspoon sugar
¾   teaspoon salt
¼   teaspoon pepper
¼   teaspoon hot sauce
½   pound small okra pods

1. Cut kernels from ears of corn; set aside.

2. Coat a nonstick skillet with cooking spray, and place over medium-high heat until hot. Add onion and bell pepper; sauté until tender. Stir in corn, tomatoes, and next 4 ingredients; arrange okra on top of corn mixture. Cover, reduce heat to low, and cook 20 minutes or until okra is tender. Yield: 6 servings (serving size: 1 cup).

POINTS: 1; **Exchanges:** 1 Starch, 1 Veg
Per serving: CAL 101 (12% from fat); PRO 3.3g; FAT 1.5g (sat 0.2g); CARB 21.8g; FIB 3.7g; CHOL 0mg; IRON 1mg; SOD 312mg; CALC 34mg

Gullah Rice

Gullah is an English-based Creole dialect spoken along the coastal regions of the Carolinas.

1   teaspoon butter or margarine
½   cup chopped celery
½   cup chopped carrot
¼   cup chopped pistachios
3   cups water
½   teaspoon salt
1   cup uncooked long-grain rice
1   tablespoon chopped fresh thyme

1. Melt butter in a medium saucepan over medium heat. Add celery, carrot, and pistachios; sauté 5 minutes or until vegetables are tender. Add water and salt; bring to a boil. Add rice and thyme; return to a boil. Cover, reduce heat, and simmer 20 minutes or until most of liquid is absorbed. Remove from heat. Let stand, covered,

10 minutes or until liquid is absorbed. Yield: 5 servings (serving size: 1 cup).

POINTS: 4; **Exchanges:** 2 Starch, ½ Fat
Per serving: CAL 186 (20% from fat); PRO 4.2g; FAT 4.2g (sat 1g); CARB 32.8g; FIB 1.7g; CHOL 2mg; IRON 2.2mg; SOD 259mg; CALC 29mg

Easy Spanish Rice

Cooking spray
½   cup chopped green bell pepper
½   cup chopped onion
2   (8-ounce) cans no-salt-added tomato sauce
1   (14½-ounce) can no-salt-added stewed tomatoes, undrained and chopped
1   cup uncooked long-grain rice
¼   cup water
1   teaspoon chili powder
½   teaspoon dried oregano
¼   teaspoon salt
¼   teaspoon ground red pepper
¼   teaspoon ground cumin

1. Coat a large nonstick skillet with cooking spray, and place over medium-high heat until hot. Add bell pepper and onion; sauté 5 minutes or until tender. Add tomato sauce and remaining ingredients; bring to a boil. Cover, reduce heat, and simmer 25 minutes or until rice is tender and liquid is absorbed. Yield: 8 servings (serving size: ½ cup).

POINTS: 2; **Exchanges:** 1½ Starch
Per serving: CAL 111 (3% from fat); PRO 2.8g; FAT 0.4g (sat 0.1g); CARB 24.4g; FIB 1.5g; CHOL 0mg; IRON 1.8mg; SOD 99mg; CALC 30mg

Easy Spanish Rice is made with pantry staples.

The best time to make Marinated Asparagus Salad is spring, when asparagus is least expensive.

Sunny Summer Squash

½ cup sliced green onions
2 teaspoons reduced-calorie stick margarine
2½ cups sliced yellow squash (about 2 medium)
1 teaspoon minced fresh or ¼ teaspoon dried oregano
⅛ teaspoon salt
⅛ teaspoon garlic powder

1. Combine green onions and margarine in a 2-quart casserole. Cover and microwave at HIGH 2 minutes, stirring after 1 minute. Add remaining ingredients; stir well. Cover and microwave at HIGH 4 minutes or until squash is crisp-tender, stirring after 2 minutes. Yield: 2 servings (serving size: 1 cup).

POINTS: 0; **Exchanges:** 2 Veg, ½ Fat
Per serving: CAL 60 (42% from fat); PRO 2.4g; FAT 2.8g (sat 0.5g); CARB 8.6g; FIB 4.8g; CHOL 0mg; IRON 1.4mg; SOD 188mg; CALC 93mg

Marinated Asparagus Salad

1½ pounds asparagus
3 tablespoons water, divided
½ cup thinly sliced green onions
2 teaspoons extra-virgin olive oil
½ teaspoon Dijon mustard
¼ teaspoon salt-free herb-and-spice blend
⅛ teaspoon salt-free lemon pepper
2 tablespoons white wine vinegar
4 Boston lettuce leaves
¼ cup chopped tomato

1. Snap off tough ends of asparagus; remove scales with a knife or vegetable peeler, if desired. Place asparagus in an 11- x 7-inch baking dish with trimmed ends toward outside of dish. Add 2 tablespoons water; cover with heavy-duty plastic wrap, and vent. Microwave at HIGH for 7 minutes or until crisp-tender. Drain asparagus, and return to dish.

2. Combine remaining 1 tablespoon water, green onions, and next 4 ingredients; stir well. Pour over asparagus, tossing gently to coat. Cover and marinate in refrigerator 3 hours.

3. Stir vinegar into asparagus mixture just before serving. Remove asparagus from marinade with tongs, reserving marinade. Divide asparagus evenly among lettuce-lined salad plates. Drizzle reserved marinade over each salad, and top with 1 tablespoon tomato. Yield: 4 servings.

Note: Vinegar will turn asparagus olive green if added earlier.

POINTS: 1; **Exchanges:** 1 Veg, ½ Fat
Per serving: CAL 55 (43% from fat); PRO 2.9g; FAT 2.6g (sat 0.4g); CARB 6.7g; FIB 2.7g; CHOL 0mg; IRON 1.2mg; SOD 27mg; CALC 34mg

Tortellini-Vegetable Toss

¼ cup hot water
1 tablespoon chopped sun-dried tomatoes, packed without oil
3 ounces uncooked fresh cheese tortellini
¼ pound asparagus, cut into ½-inch pieces
¼ cup julienne-cut zucchini
¼ cup julienne-cut carrot
1 garlic clove, minced
2 tablespoons low-salt chicken broth
¼ teaspoon olive oil
Dash of salt
Dash of freshly ground pepper
1½ teaspoons grated fresh Romano cheese

1. Combine hot water and tomatoes in a small bowl; cover and let stand 15 minutes. Drain well, and set aside.

2. Cook pasta according to package directions, omitting salt and fat; drain well.

Grilled Acorn Squash With Rosemary and Molasses-Grilled Pork Tenderloin (page 14).

3. Steam asparagus, zucchini, carrot, and garlic, covered, 5 minutes or until vegetables are crisptender. Set aside.

4. Combine chicken broth, olive oil, salt, and pepper in a large bowl; stir mixture well with a wire whisk. Add tomatoes, cooked pasta, and vegetables; toss gently. Sprinkle with grated Romano cheese, and serve immediately. Yield: 2 servings.

POINTS: 3; **Exchanges:** 1 Starch, ½ Med-fat Meat, 2 Veg
Per serving: CAL 165 (18% from fat); PRO 9.2g; FAT 3.3g (sat 1.4g); CARB 25.7g; FIB 1.9g; CHOL 22mg; IRON 1.9mg; SOD 332mg; CALC 137mg

Washington Waldorf Salad

3   cups (1-inch) diagonally sliced asparagus (about 2 pounds)
4   cups cubed Red Delicious apple (about 1¼ pounds)
2   teaspoons lemon juice
¼   cup raisins
2   tablespoons cider vinegar
1   tablespoon olive oil
2   teaspoons honey
¼   teaspoon salt
¼   teaspoon dried dill
⅛   teaspoon pepper
6   curly leaf lettuce leaves

1. Drop asparagus into a large saucepan of boiling water; cook 1 minute. Drain and plunge into ice water; drain well.

2. Combine apple and lemon juice in a bowl; toss well to coat. Add asparagus and raisins; toss well.

3. Combine vinegar and next 5 ingredients in a small bowl; stir with a whisk until well blended. Pour over salad, and toss gently. Cover and chill at least 3 hours or up to 12 hours. Serve on lettuce leaves. Yield: 6 servings (serving size: 1 cup).

POINTS: 2; **Exchanges:** 1 Fruit, 1 Veg, ½ Fat
Per serving: CAL 115 (23% from fat); PRO 2.9g; FAT 2.9g (sat 0.4g); CARB 22.8g; FIB 3.7g; CHOL 0mg; IRON 1mg; SOD 104mg; CALC 36mg

Grilled Acorn Squash With Rosemary

2 tablespoons olive oil, divided
¼ cup white wine vinegar
1 tablespoon fresh rosemary
½ teaspoon salt
4 garlic cloves, crushed
2 pounds acorn squash, cut into 24 slices
Cooking spray
Rosemary sprigs (optional)

1. Combine 1 tablespoon olive oil, white wine vinegar, 1 tablespoon fresh rosemary, salt, and garlic in a large zip-top plastic bag. Add squash slices; seal bag, and let stand 2 hours, turning bag occasionally.

2. Prepare grill. Remove squash from bag, reserving marinade. Brush remaining 1 tablespoon olive oil evenly over squash slices. Place squash slices on grill rack coated with cooking spray; cover and grill 10 minutes on each side or until tender. Place on a serving plate, and drizzle with reserved marinade. Cover and let stand 10 minutes before serving. Garnish squash with rosemary sprigs, if desired. Yield: 8 servings (serving size: 3 slices).

POINTS: 2; **Exchanges:** ½ Starch, 1 Fat
Per serving: CAL 79 (40% from fat); PRO 1g; FAT 3.5g (sat 0.5g); CARB 12.4g; FIB 1.4g; CHOL 0mg; IRON 0.6mg; SOD 151mg; CALC 33mg

Melon Salad With Orange-Honey Dressing

½ medium cantaloupe, peeled and cut into 8 slices
½ medium honeydew melon, peeled and cut into 8 slices
1 cup seedless red grapes, halved
8 Boston lettuce leaves
1 (8-ounce) carton vanilla low-fat yogurt
1 tablespoon honey
1 tablespoon thawed orange juice concentrate
Ground nutmeg (optional)

1. Divide fruit evenly among 4 lettuce-lined plates.

2. Combine yogurt, honey, and orange juice concentrate in a bowl; stir well. Drizzle ¼ cup over each salad; sprinkle with nutmeg, if desired. Yield: 4 servings.

POINTS: 3; **Exchanges:** 2 Fruit, ½ L-F Milk
Per serving: CAL 162 (8% from fat); PRO 4.6g; FAT 1.4g (sat 0.8g); CARB 36g; FIB 2.8g; CHOL 2mg; IRON 0.6mg; SOD 58mg; CALC 124mg

Roasted Potato Salad With Blue Cheese

1½ pounds small red potatoes, quartered
Olive oil-flavored cooking spray
¼ teaspoon salt
⅛ teaspoon pepper
¼ cup 1% low-fat cottage cheese
¼ cup plain fat-free yogurt

Melon Salad With Orange-Honey Dressing is sweet enough to serve for breakfast.

THE PERFECT MELON

Melons are divided into two categories: watermelons and sweet melons, such as cantaloupes and honeydew melons.

When ripe, sweet melons should give slightly when gently pressed at the blossom end. They should also smell sweet.

An unripe melon will never reach its potential, but if you accidentally purchase one, store the uncut melon in a paper bag with an apple to speed ripening.

Store cut melons in the refrigerator for no longer than three days. And, because they readily absorb odors from other foods, make sure they are stored in an airtight container.

Remove the seeds from a cantaloupe or honeydew melon with a large spoon or ice cream scoop. If only using half a melon, leave the seeds in the unused half to help keep it fresh.

1 garlic clove, minced
½ cup (2 ounces) crumbled blue cheese
½ teaspoon dried thyme
¼ teaspoon salt
¼ teaspoon freshly ground pepper
½ cup sliced green onions
¼ cup minced fresh parsley

1. Preheat oven to 400°.

2. Place potatoes in a 13- x 9-inch baking dish coated with cooking spray. Lightly coat potatoes with cooking spray; sprinkle with ¼ teaspoon salt and ⅛ teaspoon pepper. Bake at 400° for 30 minutes, stirring every 10 minutes. Spoon potatoes into a large bowl; let cool 20 minutes.

3. Place cottage cheese, yogurt, and garlic in a food processor; process until smooth. Stir in blue cheese and next 3 ingredients. Add cheese mixture, green onions, and parsley to potatoes; toss gently. Serve at room temperature or chilled. Yield: 8 servings (serving size: ½ cup).

POINTS: 2; **Exchanges:** 1 Starch, ½ Fat
Per serving: CAL 102 (21% from fat); PRO 4.8g; FAT 2.4g (sat 1.4g); CARB 15.7g; FIB 1.8g; CHOL 6mg; IRON 1.5mg; SOD 287mg; CALC 76mg

Browned Basil New Potatoes taste roasted but cook in half the time.

Browned Basil New Potatoes

2½ pounds red potatoes
2 tablespoons vegetable oil
4 garlic cloves, minced
⅓ cup thinly sliced fresh basil leaves
1 teaspoon freshly ground pepper
½ teaspoon salt

1. Cook potatoes in boiling water 15 minutes or until tender; drain. Let cool slightly, and quarter potatoes. Set aside.

2. Heat oil in a nonstick skillet over medium-high heat. Add potatoes and garlic; sauté 7 minutes or until potatoes are browned. Remove from heat. Add basil, pepper, and salt; toss gently. Yield: 10 servings (serving size: ½ cup).

POINTS: 2; **Exchanges:** 1 Starch, ½ Fat
Per serving: CAL 111 (24% from fat); PRO 2.6g; FAT 2.9g (sat 0.4g); CARB 19.5g; FIB 2.1g; CHOL 0mg; IRON 1.6mg; SOD 125mg; CALC 20mg

Spinach Salad With Chutney Dressing

¼ cup mango chutney
¼ cup low-salt chicken broth
1 tablespoon safflower or vegetable oil
2 teaspoons lemon juice
½ teaspoon curry powder
¼ teaspoon salt
4 cups torn spinach
3 cups chopped Red Delicious apple
1 large navel orange, peeled and sectioned
¾ cup diagonally sliced green onions
¼ cup sliced almonds, toasted

1. Combine first 6 ingredients in a blender or food processor; process 30 seconds or until blended.

2. Combine spinach and next 4 ingredients in a large bowl. Pour chutney mixture over salad; toss gently. Serve immediately. Yield: 8 servings (serving size: 1 cup).

POINTS: 2; **Exchanges:** 1 Fruit, ½ Fat
Per serving: CAL 90 (35% from fat); PRO 1.4g; FAT 3.5g (sat 0.3g); CARB 14.9g; FIB 2.7g; CHOL 0mg; IRON 0.8mg; SOD 101mg; CALC 37mg

Bell Pepper Salad With Feta

3 tablespoons red wine vinegar
1 tablespoon water
1½ teaspoons olive oil

½ teaspoon Dijon mustard
¾ teaspoon dried oregano
⅛ teaspoon salt
1 garlic clove, minced
¾ cup thinly sliced red onion, separated into rings
6 plum tomatoes, cut lengthwise into ⅛-inch slices
2 medium yellow bell peppers, cut into ⅛-inch rings
¼ cup (1 ounce) crumbled feta cheese
Freshly ground pepper
Oregano sprigs (optional)

1. Combine first 7 ingredients in a small bowl; stir with a whisk until well blended.

2. Combine 1 tablespoon vinegar mixture and onion rings in a medium bowl; toss well. Arrange onion rings in center of a serving platter. Arrange tomato slices around edge of platter; place bell pepper rings in center of platter on top of onion rings. Drizzle remaining vinegar mixture over vegetables. Sprinkle with crumbled feta cheese and freshly ground pepper. Garnish with oregano sprigs, if desired. Yield: 6 servings (serving size: 1 cup).

POINTS: 1; **Exchanges:** 1 Veg, ½ Fat
Per serving: CAL 56 (43% from fat); PRO 1.8g; FAT 2.7g (sat 0.9g); CARB 7.2g; FIB 1.9g; CHOL 4mg; IRON 1.1mg; SOD 119mg; CALC 36mg

Spicy Hash Browns

2 tablespoons olive oil
1 teaspoon paprika
¾ teaspoon chili powder
½ teaspoon salt
¼ teaspoon ground red pepper
⅛ teaspoon black pepper
6½ cups diced baking potato (about 2½ pounds)
Cooking spray

1. Preheat oven to 400°.

2. Combine first 6 ingredients in a large bowl; stir well. Add potatoes; stir well to coat. Place potatoes in a single layer on a jelly-roll pan coated with cooking spray. Bake at 400° for 30 minutes or until browned. Yield: 5 servings (serving size: about 1 cup).

POINTS: 6; **Exchanges:** 3½ Starch, ½ Fat
Per serving: CAL 299 (18% from fat); PRO 5.1g; FAT 5.9g (sat 0.8g); CARB 57.7g; FIB 4.4g; CHOL 0mg; IRON 3.3mg; SOD 257mg; CALC 25mg

Browned Green Beans

1½ pounds green beans
1 tablespoon vegetable oil
½ cup low-salt chicken broth
¼ teaspoon salt
⅛ teaspoon pepper
1½ tablespoons fresh lemon juice

1. Trim ends from beans; remove strings. Cut beans in half lengthwise, cutting along the string on each bean.

2. Heat oil in a large nonstick skillet over high heat. Add beans; cook 5 minutes or until lightly browned, stirring frequently. Reduce heat to medium, and gradually add broth, salt, and pepper; cook 2 minutes. Remove from heat; stir in lemon juice. Yield: 6 servings (serving size: ¾ cup).

POINTS: 1; **Exchanges:** 1 Veg, ½ Fat
Per serving: CAL 53 (42% from fat); PRO 1.9g; FAT 2.5g (sat 0.4g); CARB 7.3g; FIB 2g; CHOL 0mg; IRON 1.1mg; SOD 110mg; CALC 36mg

Bell Pepper Salad With Feta blends crisp vegetables with a tangy vinaigrette.

Indian Cauliflower

1   tablespoon light butter or margarine
1   teaspoon ground coriander
½   teaspoon curry powder
¼   teaspoon ground ginger
½   cup finely chopped onion
¼   cup ketchup
8   cups cauliflower florets
Cooking spray

1. Combine first 4 ingredients in a microwave-safe dish, and microwave at HIGH 30 seconds. Stir in onion and ketchup, and microwave at HIGH 1 minute.

2. Place cauliflower in a 2-quart casserole coated with cooking spray. Spoon onion mixture over cauliflower; toss to coat. Cover and microwave at HIGH 9 minutes, rotating dish a half-turn after 4 minutes. Yield: 6 servings (serving size: 1 cup).

POINTS: 1; **Exchanges:** 1 Veg, ½ Starch
Per serving: CAL 61 (22% from fat); PRO 3.1g; FAT 1.5g (sat 1.1g); CARB 11.2g; FIB 3.7g; CHOL 3mg; IRON 0.8mg; SOD 171mg; CALC 37mg

Citrus Romaine Salad With Strawberries

2   navel oranges
1   tablespoon sherry vinegar
1   tablespoon honey
1½ teaspoons vegetable oil
¼   teaspoon salt
⅛   to ¼ teaspoon pepper
5   cups thinly sliced romaine lettuce
1   cup halved strawberries
½   cup vertically sliced red onion

1. Peel and section oranges over a small bowl, reserving 2 tablespoons juice.

2. Combine reserved 2 tablespoons juice, vinegar, and next 4 ingredients in a small bowl; stir well with a whisk.

3. Combine orange sections, lettuce, strawberries, and onion in a large bowl; toss gently. Pour dressing over salad; toss gently to coat. Yield: 7 servings (serving size: 1 cup).

POINTS: 1; **Exchanges:** 1 Veg, ½ Fruit
Per serving: CAL 50 (22% from fat); PRO 1.2g; FAT 1.2g (sat 0.2g); CARB 9.3g; FIB 2.5g; CHOL 0mg; IRON 0.6mg; SOD 100mg; CALC 31mg

Oven-Fried Sweet Potatoes

4   medium sweet potatoes, peeled and cut into ¼-inch slices (about 1½ pounds)
1   tablespoon olive oil
¼   teaspoon salt
¼   teaspoon pepper
Cooking spray
1   tablespoon finely chopped fresh parsley
1   teaspoon grated orange rind
1   small garlic clove, minced

1. Preheat oven to 400°.

2. Combine first 4 ingredients in a large bowl, and toss gently to coat. Arrange sweet potato slices in a single layer on a large baking sheet coated with cooking spray. Bake at 400° for 30 minutes or until tender, turning potato slices after 15 minutes.

3. Combine parsley, orange rind, and garlic in a small bowl; stir well. Sprinkle parsley mixture over sweet potato slices. Yield: 7 servings (serving size: ½ cup).

POINTS: 2; **Exchanges:** 1½ Starch
Per serving: CAL 122 (18% from fat); PRO 1.6g; FAT 2.4g (sat 0.3g); CARB 23.9g; FIB 3g; CHOL 0mg; IRON 0.6mg; SOD 97mg; CALC 24mg

Broccoli-and-Walnut Sauté

1½ pounds broccoli
½   cup water
2   tablespoons balsamic vinegar
2   teaspoons cornstarch
1   teaspoon chicken-flavored bouillon granules
2   teaspoons vegetable oil
1   cup vertically sliced onion
½   cup red bell pepper strips
1   garlic clove, minced
¼   cup chopped walnuts, toasted

1. Trim off large leaves of broccoli, and remove tough ends of lower stalks. Cut broccoli into florets. Peel broccoli stems, and thinly slice. Set broccoli aside.

2. Combine water and next 3 ingredients in a small bowl; stir well, and set aside.

3. Heat oil in a large nonstick skillet over medium heat. Add broccoli, onion, bell pepper, and garlic; sauté 3 minutes or until broccoli is

Serve Pasta With Gremolata as a side to lamb or veal.

crisp-tender. Add cornstarch mixture; bring to a boil, and cook 1 minute, stirring constantly. Spoon into a serving bowl; sprinkle with walnuts. Yield: 6 servings.

POINTS: 1; **Exchanges:** 2 Veg, 1 Fat
Per serving: CAL 94 (43% from fat); PRO 4.6g; FAT 5.1g (sat 0.4g); CARB 10.5g; FIB 4.3g; CHOL 0mg; IRON 1.4mg; SOD 33mg; CALC 65mg

Pasta With Gremolata

Gremolata, a combination of parsley, lemon, and garlic, adds a sprightly taste to meats and side dishes.

½   cup finely chopped fresh parsley
½   teaspoon grated lemon rind
2   large garlic cloves, minced
1   tablespoon extra-virgin olive oil, divided
1   (14½-ounce) can plum tomatoes, undrained and chopped
1   tablespoon chopped fresh basil
3   cups hot cooked penne (about 1⅓ cups uncooked short tubular pasta)
Parsley sprigs (optional)

1. Combine first 3 ingredients in a bowl; stir well, and set aside.

2. Heat 1½ teaspoons olive oil in a nonstick skillet over medium heat. Add tomatoes; bring to a boil, and cook 10 minutes. Remove from heat; stir in basil.

3. Combine pasta and remaining 1½ teaspoons oil in a bowl; toss well. Add parsley mixture and tomato mixture; toss gently. Serve warm. Garnish with parsley sprigs, if desired. Yield: 4 servings (serving size: ¾ cup).

POINTS: 4; **Exchanges:** 2 Starch, 1 Fat
Per serving: CAL 198 (20% from fat); PRO 6g; FAT 4.5g (sat 0.6g); CARB 34.3g; FIB 2.8g; CHOL 0mg; IRON 2.6mg; SOD 15mg; CALC 48mg

Cavatappi With Spinach,
Beans, and Asiago Cheese

Vegetarian Entrées

EARTH'S BOUNTY PROVIDES PLENTY OF
RECIPES FOR THE MEATLESS MEAL.
HERE ARE OUR FAVORITES.

Usually eaten for brunch,
Eggs Sardou may be
served as a light lunch
or dinner.

Cavatappi With Spinach, Beans, and Asiago Cheese

If you toss the spinach and the Asiago cheese while the pasta is still warm, the spinach will wilt and the cheese will soften. Then, the flavors will blend and become more pungent.

8   cups coarsely chopped spinach leaves
4   cups hot cooked cavatappi (about 6 ounces uncooked spiral-shaped pasta)
2   tablespoons olive oil
¼   teaspoon salt
¼   teaspoon pepper
1   (19-ounce) can cannellini beans or other white beans, rinsed and drained
2   garlic cloves, crushed
½   cup (2 ounces) shredded Asiago cheese
Freshly ground pepper (optional)

1. Combine all ingredients in a large bowl; toss well. Sprinkle with freshly ground pepper, if desired. Yield: 4 servings (serving size: 2 cups).

POINTS: 8; **Exchanges:** 3½ Starch, 1 Veg, 1½ Fat, 1 Very Lean Meat
Per serving: CAL 401 (27% from fat); FAT12g (sat 3.4g); PRO 18.8g; CARB 54.7g; FIB 6.7g; CHOL 10mg; IRON 6.4mg; SOD 464mg; CALC 306mg

Eggs Sardou

This egg and artichoke dish is named after a famous nineteenth-century French playwright, Victorien Sardou.

1   tablespoon all-purpose flour
¾   cup 1% low-fat milk
⅓   cup fat-free sour cream
2   tablespoons grated Parmesan cheese
¼   teaspoon salt
⅛   teaspoon pepper
1   (10-ounce) package frozen chopped spinach, thawed, drained, and squeezed dry
2   large eggs
Cooking spray
2   canned artichoke bottoms, thinly sliced crosswise
2   teaspoons grated Parmesan cheese

1. Place flour in a small saucepan. Gradually add milk, stirring with a whisk until blended. Add sour cream, 2 tablespoons cheese, salt, pepper, and spinach; stir well. Place over medium heat; cook 8 minutes or until mixture is thick, stirring occasionally (do not boil). Remove from heat, and keep warm.

2. Add water to a large skillet, filling two-thirds full; bring to a simmer. Break eggs into each of 2 (6-ounce) custard cups coated with cooking spray. Place custard cups in simmering water in skillet; cover skillet, and cook 6 minutes or until eggs are done. Remove custard cups from water; set aside.

3. Spoon ½ cup spinach mixture into each of 2 individual gratin dishes; fan artichoke bottoms over spinach mixture. Invert poached eggs onto artichoke; top each egg with ¼ cup spinach mixture. Sprinkle each dish with 1 teaspoon Parmesan cheese. Place gratin dishes on a baking sheet; broil 3 minutes. Yield: 2 servings.

POINTS: 4; **Exchanges:** 2 Veg, 1 Sk Milk, 1 Med-fat Meat
Per serving: CAL 232 (32% from fat); PRO 19.4g; FAT 8.3g (sat 3.2g); CARB 20.7g; FIB 5.1g; CHOL 220mg; IRON 4.5mg; SOD 655mg; CALC 383mg

Bean-and-Green Chile Quesadillas

1   cup drained canned Great Northern beans
½   teaspoon ground cumin
8   (8-inch) flour tortillas
4   teaspoons chopped pickled jalapeño peppers
½   cup canned chopped green chiles
¼   cup drained canned black beans
8   (⅛-inch-thick) slices tomato
¾   cup (3 ounces) shredded reduced-fat sharp cheddar cheese
4   teaspoons minced fresh cilantro
1   (8-ounce) carton plain low-fat yogurt
Cooking spray

1. Combine Great Northern beans and cumin in a small bowl; stir well.

2. Place ¼ cup bean mixture on each of 4 tortillas, and mash with a fork to within ½ inch of edges. Sprinkle each tortilla with 1 teaspoon jalapeños, 2 tablespoons green chiles, and 1 tablespoon black beans. Top each one with 2 tomato slices, 3 tablespoons cheese, 1 teaspoon cilantro, and another tortilla.

3. Spoon yogurt onto several layers of heavy-duty paper towels; spread to ½-inch thickness. Cover with additional paper towels; let stand 5 minutes. Scrape yogurt cheese into a bowl using a rubber spatula; set aside.

4. Coat a large nonstick skillet with cooking spray; place over medium-high heat until hot. Add 1 quesadilla; cook 3 minutes on each side or until golden. Remove quesadilla from skillet; set aside, and keep warm. Repeat procedure with remaining quesadillas. Cut each quesadilla into 4 wedges. Serve warm with yogurt cheese.

Use your favorite beans in Bean-and-Green Chile Quesadillas.

QUESADILLAS: A WORLD OF POSSIBILITIES

Quesadillas, traditional Mexican snack food, come in all flavors. Fruit quesadillas, fish quesadillas, beef quesadillas—imagine a filling and it has been spread on a tortilla and fried.

Our version takes advantage of a classic bean and cheese mixture, adding fresh vegetables and piquant chiles for extra flavor. And, unlike most quesadilla recipes, this one calls for cooking spray and a nonstick skillet, not lots of hot oil, for cooking.

Many people treat quesadillas as appetizers, but we made this version hearty enough for a meatless entrée. Individual wedges do make good appetizers though—one-fourth of a quesadilla contains only 125 calories. If you don't have time to make the yogurt cheese, fat-free sour cream will work.

Yield: 4 servings (serving size: 1 quesadilla and 1 tablespoon yogurt cheese).

POINTS: 10; Exchanges: 5 Starch, ½ Very Lean Meat, ½ Med-fat Meat, 1 Fat
Per serving: CAL 498 (22% from fat); FAT 12.2g (sat 4.1g); PRO 23.6g; CARB 74.2g; FIB 6g; CHOL 18mg; IRON 5.1mg; SOD 826mg; CALC 457mg

Fresh Corn-and-Pasta Frittata

1¼ cups egg substitute
¼   cup dry breadcrumbs
¼   cup (1 ounce) shredded provolone cheese
1   teaspoon olive oil
1   cup chopped green onions
1   cup presliced mushrooms
¾   cup fresh corn kernels (about 1 ear)
1   cup cooked angel hair pasta (about
     2 ounces uncooked pasta)
¼   cup grated Parmesan cheese
Green onions (optional)

1. Preheat oven to 450°.

2. Combine first 3 ingredients in a small bowl; stir well, and set aside.

3. Wrap handle of a nonstick skillet with foil. Heat oil in skillet over medium-high heat. Add onions, mushrooms, and corn; sauté 4 minutes or until tender. Add pasta; stir well. Add egg substitute mixture; cook 2 minutes or until set around edges (do not stir). Sprinkle with Parmesan cheese. Bake at 450° for 5 minutes or until center is set. Garnish with onions, if desired. Yield: 2 servings.

POINTS: 8; Exchanges: 2½ Very Lean Meat, 3 Starch, 1 Veg, ½ Fat, ½ Med-fat Meat
Per serving: CAL 416 (23% from fat); FAT 10.6g (sat 5g); PRO 31.2g; CARB 50.4g; FIB 4.8g; CHOL 18mg; IRON 6mg; SOD 664mg; CALC 368mg

Herbed-Potato Frittata

2   cups diced red potato
1   tablespoon reduced-calorie stick margarine
⅓   cup sliced green onions
1   teaspoon dried basil
½   teaspoon dried marjoram
¼   teaspoon salt
¼   teaspoon pepper
1   garlic clove, minced
2   (8-ounce) cartons egg substitute
¾   cup (3 ounces) shredded reduced-fat sharp
     cheddar cheese

1. Place potato in a saucepan; add water to cover, and bring to a boil. Cover, reduce heat, and simmer 15 minutes or until tender; drain.

2. Melt margarine in a 10-inch nonstick skillet over medium-high heat. Add potato, green onions, and next 5 ingredients; sauté 2 minutes. Spread mixture evenly in bottom of skillet; pour egg substitute over potato mixture. Reduce heat to medium-low, and cook, uncovered, 8 minutes or until almost set. Wrap handle of skillet with aluminum foil; broil 3 minutes. Sprinkle with cheese; broil an additional 30 seconds or until cheese melts. Yield: 4 servings.

POINTS: 6; Exchanges: 2 Very Lean Meat, 1½ Starch, 1 Med-fat Meat
Per serving: CAL 274 (24% from fat); PRO 25.6g; FAT 7.4g (sat 3.5g); CARB 26.1g; FIB 2g; CHOL 19mg; IRON 3.6mg; SOD 681mg; CALC 331mg

New England Beans and Brown Bread

This cylindrical loaf of sweet bread is packaged in a can and sold in large supermarkets.

½   teaspoon olive oil
2   cups chopped onion
2   garlic cloves, minced
1   cup apple cider
½   cup ketchup
3   tablespoons maple syrup
2   tablespoons balsamic vinegar
½   teaspoon dried savory
½   teaspoon dry mustard
½   teaspoon ground cumin
2   (16-ounce) cans navy beans, drained
8   (½-inch) slices New England-style brown
     bread with raisins

1. Heat oil in a Dutch oven over medium-high heat. Add onion and garlic; sauté 3 minutes or until tender. Stir in cider and next 7 ingredients; bring to a boil. Reduce heat, and simmer, uncovered, 30 minutes. Serve beans with brown bread. Yield: 4 servings (serving size: 1 cup beans and 2 slices bread).

POINTS: 10; Exchanges: 1 Very Lean Meat, 6 Starch, 1½ Fruit
Per serving: CAL 599 (4% from fat); FAT 2.6g (sat 0.3g); PRO 18.8g; CARB 126.8g; FIB 11.5g; CHOL 0mg; IRON 4.8g; SOD 1,492mg; CALC 120mg

Portobello mushrooms give Mushroom-Swiss Stuffed Potatoes a beef-like taste and texture.

Mushroom-Swiss Stuffed Potatoes

6   (8-ounce) baking potatoes
2   teaspoons olive oil
2   cups quartered mushrooms
2   cups (½-inch) diced portobello mushrooms
1   cup sliced shiitake mushroom caps
¼   cup finely chopped onion
2   garlic cloves, minced
2   tablespoons all-purpose flour
½   teaspoon salt
⅛   teaspoon white pepper
1   cup skim milk
1   tablespoon dry sherry
1   cup (4 ounces) shredded Swiss cheese

1. Preheat oven to 375°.

2. Wrap potatoes in foil; bake at 375° for 1 hour or until tender.

3. Heat oil in a large nonstick skillet over medium heat. Add mushrooms, onion, and garlic; sauté 2 minutes. Stir in flour, salt, and white pepper. Gradually add milk and sherry, stirring with a whisk until blended. Cook 2 minutes or until thick and bubbly. Add cheese; cook 1 minute or until cheese melts, stirring constantly.

4. Unwrap potatoes. Split open each potato; fluff pulp with a fork. Spoon ⅓ cup mushroom sauce into center of each potato. Place potatoes on a baking sheet; broil 4 minutes or until sauce begins to brown. Yield: 6 servings.

Note: You can substitute any combination of exotic and domestic mushrooms to measure 5 cups.

POINTS: 6; **Exchanges:** 3 Starch, 1 Veg, ½ Hi-fat Meat
Per serving: CAL 312 (21% from fat); FAT 7.3g (sat 3.7g); PRO 13.9g; CARB 49.9g; FIB 5g; CHOL 18mg; IRON 3.9mg; SOD 286mg; CALC 271mg

Spinach-Mushroom Pizza

To save time, thaw and drain spinach in advance.

Cooking spray
2   tablespoons cornmeal
1   (10-ounce) can refrigerated pizza crust dough
1   (10-ounce) package frozen chopped spinach, thawed, drained, and squeezed dry

¾ cup (3 ounces) shredded part-skim
   mozzarella cheese
1 teaspoon dried Italian seasoning
2 teaspoons bottled minced garlic
¼ teaspoon pepper
1 (4.5-ounce) jar sliced mushrooms, drained
2 (14½-ounce) cans pasta-style tomatoes,
   drained
½ cup (2 ounces) crumbled feta cheese

1. Preheat oven to 425°.

2. Coat a 15- x 10-inch jelly-roll pan with cooking spray; sprinkle with cornmeal. Unroll pizza
dough, and press dough into pan. Bake at 425°
for 6 minutes or just until crust begins to brown.

3. Combine spinach, mozzarella cheese, Italian
seasoning, garlic, and pepper in a bowl; stir well.
Spread spinach mixture over crust, leaving a
½-inch border. Top with mushrooms and tomatoes; sprinkle with feta cheese. Bake at 425° for 9
minutes or until crust is lightly browned (feta
cheese will not melt). Cut into 6 equal pieces.
Yield: 6 servings.

POINTS: 5; **Exchanges**: ½ Med-fat Meat, 1 Veg, 2 Starch, 1 Fat
Per serving: CAL 263 (21% from fat); PRO 9.4g; FAT 6g (sat 3.4g);
CARB 33.1g; FIB 4.3g; CHOL 17mg; IRON 1.6mg; SOD 1,154mg;
CALC 202mg

Smashed Potato-and-Broccoli Casserole

While most potato casseroles are served as side
dishes, this one has enough protein to be served
as a main dish.

2 pounds baking potatoes, halved
1 cup chopped broccoli
½ cup diced onion
½ cup part-skim ricotta cheese
1½ teaspoons chopped fresh or ½ teaspoon
   dried dill
½ teaspoon salt
⅛ teaspoon ground red pepper
1 (8-ounce) carton fat-free sour cream
Cooking spray
¾ cup (3 ounces) shredded reduced-fat sharp
   cheddar cheese

1. Preheat oven to 375°.

2. Place potatoes in a saucepan; cover with water.
Bring to a boil. Reduce heat; simmer 20 minutes
or until tender. Drain potatoes in a colander over

a bowl, reserving 1 cup cooking liquid. Return
potatoes and reserved 1 cup liquid to pan; mash
with a potato masher until slightly chunky.

3. Add chopped broccoli and next 6 ingredients to
pan; stir well. Spoon potato mixture into an 11- x
7-inch baking dish coated with cooking spray;
bake at 375° for 35 minutes. Sprinkle with cheddar cheese; bake an additional 5 minutes or until
cheese melts. Yield: 6 servings (serving size: 1 cup).

POINTS: 6; **Exchanges**: 3 Starch, ½ Med-fat Meat
Per serving: CAL 292 (17% from fat); FAT 5.6g (sat 3.2g);
PRO14.9g; CARB 45.5g; FIB 3.9g; CHOL 19mg; IRON 2.5mg; SOD
405mg; CALC 257mg

Couscous With Corn and Black Beans

1½ cups water
1 cup uncooked couscous
½ cup chopped fresh parsley
1 (15-ounce) can black beans, rinsed and
   drained
1 (10-ounce) package frozen whole-kernel
   corn, thawed and drained
3 tablespoons orange juice
1 teaspoon grated lemon rind
3 tablespoons fresh lemon juice
2 tablespoons olive oil
¼ teaspoon salt
¼ teaspoon ground cumin
⅛ teaspoon coarsely ground pepper

1. Bring water to a boil in a medium saucepan,
and stir in couscous. Remove from heat; cover
and let stand 5 minutes. Fluff with a fork.

To round out the meal,
serve a fruit salad and
French bread with
Smashed Potato-and-
Broccoli Casserole.

2. Combine couscous, parsley, beans, and corn in a large bowl; toss well. Combine orange juice and next 6 ingredients in a small bowl; stir well. Add to couscous mixture; toss well. Yield: 4 servings (serving size: 1¼ cups).

POINTS: 6; **Exchanges:** 3½ Starch, 1 Fat
Per serving: CAL 332 (21% from fat); PRO 12.4g; FAT 7.6g (sat 1g); CARB 58g; FIB 6g; CHOL 0mg; IRON 2.8mg; SOD 321mg; CALC 32mg

Eggs Pipérade With Roasted Potatoes

Pipérade is a dish from the Basque region of France that always includes tomatoes and bell peppers. This version with eggs is similar to a frittata.

1   teaspoon olive oil
¾   cup chopped red bell pepper
¾   cup chopped green bell pepper
1   garlic clove, minced
1   (14.5-ounce) can diced tomatoes, undrained
½   teaspoon dried thyme
¼   teaspoon salt
¼   to ½ teaspoon ground red pepper
4   large eggs, lightly beaten
1   tablespoon chopped fresh parsley (optional)

1. Heat oil in a large nonstick skillet over medium-high heat. Add bell peppers and garlic; sauté 5 minutes. Add tomatoes, thyme, salt, and ground red pepper; cover, reduce heat to medium, and cook 7 minutes or until bell peppers are tender. Uncover and cook 1 minute or until most of liquid evaporates. Gently stir in eggs; cover and cook 3 minutes or until set (do not stir). Cut into wedges. Garnish with parsley, if desired. Yield: 4 servings.

POINTS: 3; **Exchanges:** 2 Veg, 1 Med-fat Meat
Per serving: CAL 134 (46% from fat); FAT 6.8g (sat 1.8g); PRO 8.1g; CARB 10.7g; FIB 1.4g; CHOL 221mg; IRON 2.2mg; SOD 476mg; CALC 67mg

Greek White Bean Risotto

4½ cups low-salt chicken broth
Cooking spray
1   tablespoon minced garlic
1   cup uncooked Arborio rice or other short-grain rice
1   teaspoon dried oregano
¾   cup drained canned Great Northern beans
¼   cup diced sun-dried tomatoes, packed without oil
¼   cup sliced ripe olives
1   (4-ounce) package feta cheese with basil and tomato, finely crumbled
¼   cup (1 ounce) grated fresh Parmesan cheese

1. Bring broth to a simmer in a medium saucepan (do not boil). Keep warm over low heat.

2. Coat a large saucepan with cooking spray; place over medium-high heat until hot. Add garlic; sauté 1 minute. Stir in rice and oregano. Reduce heat to medium-low. Add 1 cup broth; cook until broth is nearly absorbed, stirring constantly. Add ½ cup broth; cook until broth is nearly absorbed, stirring constantly. Stir in beans, tomatoes, and olives. Add remaining broth, ½ cup at a time, stirring constantly; cook until each portion of broth is absorbed before adding the next (about 25 minutes). Remove from heat; add cheeses, stirring until cheeses melt. Yield: 5 servings.

POINTS: 7; **Exchanges:** 3½ Starch, ½ Med-fat Meat, ½ Fat
Per serving: CAL 342 (24% from fat); PRO 14g; FAT 9.2g (sat 5g); CARB 51.1g; FIB 2.6g; CHOL 24mg; IRON 4.4mg; SOD 680mg; CALC 220mg

Vegetable Pilaf

Using only half the seasoning packet from the rice mix reduces the sodium in this recipe without sacrificing the flavor.

1½ cups frozen whole-kernel corn, thawed
3   shallots, thinly sliced
2   teaspoons vegetable oil
Cooking spray
1   (6-ounce) package long-grain and wild rice mix (such as Uncle Ben's)
½   cup dried apricots, cut into thin strips
2   tablespoons chopped fresh parsley
1   (15-ounce) can no-salt-added chickpeas (garbanzo beans), drained
2   tablespoons balsamic vinegar
2   tablespoons orange juice
⅛   teaspoon pepper

1. Preheat oven to 375°.

2. Combine first 3 ingredients in a 2-quart casserole coated with cooking spray; stir well. Bake,

Eggs Pipérade With
Roasted Potatoes

uncovered, at 375° for 30 minutes or until tender, stirring after 15 minutes. Spoon into a large bowl; set aside.

3. Cook rice according to package directions, omitting fat and using only half the contents of seasoning packet (discard remainder of packet).

4. Add cooked rice, apricots, parsley, and chickpeas to corn mixture; toss well. Combine vinegar, orange juice, and pepper; drizzle over rice mixture; toss gently. Serve immediately. Yield: 4 servings (serving size: 1½ cups).

POINTS: 7; **Exchanges:** 4½ Starch, ½ Fruit, ½ Fat
Per serving: CAL 395 (10% from fat); PRO 13.5g; FAT 4.3g (sat 0.4g); CARB 78.9g; FIB 8.3g; CHOL 0mg; IRON 3.7mg; SOD 255mg; CALC 66mg

Using a prepared polenta takes most of the work out of Polenta With Roasted Red Peppers and Fontina Cheese.

Polenta With Roasted Red Peppers and Fontina Cheese

3 large red bell peppers
1 (14.5-ounce) can whole tomatoes, undrained

Cooking spray
1 (16-ounce) package refrigerated prepared polenta, cut into 12 slices
1¼ cups (5 ounces) shredded fontina cheese
Fresh basil (optional)

1. Cut peppers in half lengthwise; discard seeds and membranes. Place pepper halves, skin sides up, on foil-lined baking sheet; flatten with hand. Broil 10 minutes or until blackened. Place in a zip-top plastic bag; seal. Let stand 15 minutes. Peel; cut into strips. Set aside.

2. Preheat oven to 350°.

3. Drain tomatoes, reserving liquid. Chop tomatoes. Place a large skillet over medium-low heat until hot. Add chopped tomatoes, and cook 1 minute. Gradually add tomato liquid, and cook 1 minute. Add roasted pepper strips, and cook 5 minutes.

4. Spread ¼ cup tomato mixture in bottom of a 13- x 9-inch baking dish coated with cooking

spray. Arrange polenta slices over tomato mixture; spread remaining tomato mixture over polenta. Sprinkle with cheese. Bake at 350° for 25 minutes. Garnish with basil, if desired. Yield: 6 servings.

POINTS: 4; Exchanges: 1 Veg, 1 Starch, 1 Med-fat Meat
Per serving: CAL 187 (38% from fat); FAT 7.8g (sat 4.6g); PRO 9.2g; CARB 20.2g; FIB 3.4g; CHOL 27mg; IRON 2.4mg; SOD 622mg; CALC 151mg

Curried Chickpeas and Black Beans

2 teaspoons vegetable oil
1 cup chopped onion
1 tablespoon peeled minced fresh ginger
2 teaspoons curry powder
1 (14.5-ounce) can diced tomatoes, undrained
⅛ teaspoon salt
1 (15-ounce) can black beans, rinsed and drained
1 (15-ounce) can chickpeas (garbanzo beans), rinsed and drained
⅓ cup chopped fresh parsley
1 tablespoon lemon juice

1. Heat oil in a large nonstick skillet over medium heat. Add onion and ginger, and sauté 3 minutes or until tender. Stir in curry powder, and cook 1 minute. Add tomatoes, and cook 1 minute or until mixture is slightly thick, stirring occasionally. Add salt, black beans, and chickpeas; stir well. Cover, reduce heat, and simmer 5 minutes. Remove from heat, and stir in fresh parsley and lemon juice. Serve warm. Yield: 4 servings (serving size: 1 cup).

POINTS: 4; Exchanges: ½ Very Lean Meat, 3 Starch
Per serving: CAL 258 (17% from fat); PRO 13.3g; FAT 4.9g (sat 0.8g); CARB 43.2g; FIB 7.1g; CHOL 0mg; IRON 4.6mg; SOD 552mg; CALC 100mg

Tofu Piccata

2 (10.5-ounce) packages extra-firm tofu, drained and cut into 1-inch cubes
1 tablespoon lemon juice
⅓ cup cornstarch
¼ cup grated Parmesan cheese
¼ cup dry breadcrumbs
1 tablespoon minced fresh parsley
1 teaspoon dried Italian seasoning
3 large egg whites
Cooking spray
4 cups hot cooked linguine (about 8 ounces uncooked pasta)
2 cups bottled marinara sauce, warmed
1 tablespoon capers
Lemon wedges (optional)

1. Place tofu cubes and lemon juice in a large zip-top plastic bag; seal bag, and shake gently to coat. Add cornstarch to bag; seal bag, and shake gently to coat. Let stand 1 hour.

2. Combine Parmesan cheese, breadcrumbs, parsley, and Italian seasoning in another large zip-top plastic bag; seal bag, and shake well. Place egg whites in a shallow bowl, and stir well. Dip tofu cubes into egg whites, and add to cheese mixture in bag; seal bag, and shake gently to coat.

3. Coat a large nonstick skillet with cooking spray, and place over medium heat until hot. Add tofu cubes, and cook 8 minutes or until browned, turning occasionally.

4. Spoon pasta onto individual plates, and top with tofu cubes. Spoon marinara sauce evenly over tofu and pasta, and sprinkle with capers. Serve with lemon wedges, if desired. Yield: 4 servings (serving size: 1 cup pasta, 1 cup tofu, ½ cup marinara sauce, and ¾ teaspoon capers).

POINTS: 10; Exchanges: 2 Med-fat Meat, 4 Starch, 1 Veg
Per serving: CAL 495 (27% from fat); PRO 26.1g; FAT 14.6g (sat 2.9g); CARB 69.2g; FIB 5.2g; CHOL 4mg; IRON 11.9mg; SOD 1,229mg; CALC 287mg

Vegetarian Paella

Here's a takeoff on the classic Spanish dish of saffron-flavored rice, minus the shellfish, chicken, and sausage. If you want to stick with tradition, include grilled shrimp or fish in the menu.

Cooking spray
⅔ cup chopped onion
⅔ cup diced red bell pepper
2 garlic cloves, minced
1 cup frozen artichoke hearts, thawed
3 cups torn fresh spinach
½ cup water
2 (10½-ounce) cans low-salt chicken broth

1¼ cups uncooked jasmine rice
¾ teaspoon salt
½ teaspoon Hungarian sweet paprika
¼ teaspoon saffron threads
1 cup frozen baby lima beans, thawed
⅓ cup frozen green peas, thawed

1. Coat a large saucepan with cooking spray, and place over medium-high heat until hot. Add onion, bell pepper, and garlic; sauté 3 minutes. Add artichokes; sauté 2 minutes.

2. Add spinach, water, and broth; bring to a boil. Add rice and next 3 ingredients, and stir well. Cover, reduce heat, and simmer 15 minutes. Stir in lima beans and peas; cover and cook an additional 10 minutes or until liquid is absorbed. Remove from heat, and let stand, covered, 5 minutes. Fluff with a fork. Yield: 4 servings (serving size: 1¾ cups).

POINTS: 6; **Exchanges:** 4½ Starch
Per serving: CAL 348 (5% from fat); PRO 11.9g; FAT 2.1g (sat 0.5g); CARB 71.1g; FIB 6.5g; CHOL 0mg; IRON 5.5mg; SOD 607mg; CALC 97mg

Artichoke-Stuffed Tomatoes

4 large tomatoes
¾ cup diced yellow squash
⅓ cup (1⅓ ounces) shredded part-skim mozzarella cheese
¼ cup chopped fresh parsley
¼ cup dry breadcrumbs
¼ cup grated Parmesan cheese
1 tablespoon sliced green onions
1 teaspoon dried basil
1 teaspoon olive oil
¼ teaspoon dried Italian seasoning
1 (14-ounce) can artichoke hearts, drained and sliced

1. Preheat oven to 350°.

2. Cut a ¼-inch slice from stem end of each tomato, and discard stem ends. Scoop out pulp, leaving tomato shells intact. Reserve pulp for another use. Invert tomato shells on paper towels to drain.

3. Combine squash and next 9 ingredients in a bowl, and stir well. Spoon squash mixture evenly into tomato shells. Place tomatoes in a 9-inch square baking pan. Bake at 350° for 45 minutes or until thoroughly heated. Yield: 2 servings.

POINTS: 6; **Exchanges:** 1 Hi-fat Meat, 2 Starch, 2 Veg
Per serving: CAL 313 (30% from fat); PRO 18.3g; FAT 10.4g (sat 4.5g); CARB 43.3g; FIB 7.4g; CHOL 19mg; IRON 5mg; SOD 831mg; CALC 393mg

Spinach, Rice, and Feta Pie

2 teaspoons margarine
¾ cup chopped onion
2 teaspoons all-purpose flour
½ teaspoon salt
¼ teaspoon pepper
1½ cups 1% low-fat milk
2 cups cooked long-grain rice
¾ cup (3 ounces) crumbled feta cheese
1 large egg, lightly beaten
2 large egg whites
1 (10-ounce) package frozen chopped spinach, thawed, drained, and squeezed dry
Olive oil-flavored cooking spray
2 tablespoons grated Parmesan cheese

1. Preheat oven to 400°.

2. Melt margarine in a large saucepan over medium heat. Add onion, and sauté 3 minutes. Stir in flour, salt, and pepper. Gradually add milk, stirring with a whisk until well blended. Bring mixture to a simmer, and cook 1 minute or until slightly thick, stirring constantly. Remove from heat, and stir in rice, feta cheese, egg, egg whites, and spinach.

3. Pour mixture into a 9-inch pie plate coated with cooking spray. Sprinkle Parmesan cheese over pie. Bake at 400° for 35 minutes or until set. Broil 2 minutes or until pie is golden brown. Yield: 6 servings.

POINTS: 4; **Exchanges:** 1½ Starch, 1 Med-fat Meat
Per serving: CAL 198 (30% from fat); FAT 6.7g (sat 3.4g); PRO 10g; CARB 24.8g; FIB 2.3g; CHOL 53mg; IRON 1.9mg; SOD 494mg; CALC 237mg

Spanish Omelets

1½ cups sliced potato
½ cup chopped onion
½ cup chopped red bell pepper

1 garlic clove, minced
¼ cup sliced pitted manzanilla or green olives
1 tablespoon minced fresh or 1 teaspoon dried oregano
½ cup (2 ounces) shredded part-skim mozzarella cheese
8 large egg whites
4 large eggs
¼ teaspoon salt
⅛ teaspoon pepper
Cooking spray
½ teaspoon olive oil, divided

1. Place potato slices in a medium saucepan, and cover with water. Bring to a boil; reduce heat. Simmer 15 minutes or until tender; drain. Let cool; dice, and set aside.

2. Place a medium nonstick skillet over medium heat until hot. Add onion, bell pepper, and garlic; sauté 8 minutes. Add diced potato, olives, and oregano; cook 1 minute or until thoroughly heated. Remove from heat, and stir in mozzarella cheese. Set aside.

3. Combine egg whites, eggs, salt, and pepper in a bowl; stir well with a whisk.

4. Coat a small nonstick skillet with cooking spray; add ¼ teaspoon olive oil, and place over medium-high heat until hot. Add half of egg mixture to skillet; cook 2 minutes or until egg begins to set (do not stir). Carefully lift edges of omelet with a spatula, allowing uncooked egg to flow under omelet. Cook 3 minutes; turn omelet over. Spoon 1 cup potato mixture onto half of omelet; fold omelet in half. Cook an additional 1 minute. Slide omelet onto a plate; set aside, and keep warm. Repeat procedure with remaining ingredients. Yield: 4 servings (serving size: ½ omelet).

Note: Substitute 2 cups egg substitute for 8 egg whites and 4 eggs, if desired.

POINTS: 5; **Exchanges:** 1 Starch, ½ Fat, 1 Med-fat Meat, 1 Very Lean Meat
Per serving: CAL 213 (38% from fat); FAT 9.1g (sat 3.3g); PRO 18.1g; CARB 14.5g; FIB 1.7g; CHOL 229mg; IRON 2mg; SOD 462mg; CALC 157mg

Olives give Spanish Omelets a rich flavor.

Soups and Sandwiches

FEW COUPLES HAVE LASTED AS LONG
AS THIS CLASSIC DUO. MAYBE
OPPOSITES DO MORE THAN ATTRACT.

Cheddar Chicken Chowder

Cheddar Chicken Chowder

Preparing this chowder takes very little effort when you purchase skinned, boned chicken breasts and shredded cheese.

Cooking spray
2 bacon slices
1 pound skinned, boned chicken breasts, cut into bite-size pieces
1 cup chopped onion
1 cup diced red bell pepper
2 garlic cloves, minced
4½ cups fat-free chicken broth
1¾ cups peeled diced red potato
2¼ cups frozen whole-kernel corn
½ cup all-purpose flour
2 cups 2% reduced-fat milk
¾ cup (3 ounces) shredded cheddar cheese
½ teaspoon salt
¼ teaspoon pepper

1. Coat a Dutch oven with cooking spray; add bacon, and cook over medium-high heat until bacon is crisp. Remove bacon from pan, reserving bacon fat in pan. Crumble bacon; set aside. Add chicken, onion, bell pepper, and garlic to bacon fat in pan; sauté 5 minutes. Add broth and potato; bring to boil. Cover, reduce heat, and simmer 20 minutes or until potato is tender. Add corn; stir well.

2. Place flour in a medium bowl. Gradually add milk, stirring with a whisk until blended. Add milk mixture to soup, and cook over medium heat 15 minutes or until thick, stirring frequently. Remove from heat; stir in cheese, salt, and pepper. Top with crumbled bacon. Yield: 7 servings (serving size: 1½ cups).

POINTS: 6; **Exchanges:** 2 Starch, 3 Very Lean Meat, 1 Fat
Per serving: CAL 306 (22% from fat); PRO 25g; FAT 7.5g (sat 4g); CARB 33.7g; FIB 2.9g; CHOL 58mg; IRON 1.6mg; SOD 376mg; CALC 193mg

Potato-Broccoli Cheese Soup

Cooking spray
1 cup chopped onion
3 cups peeled cubed baking potato (about 1¼ pounds)
1½ cups 1% low-fat milk
1 (14¼-ounce) can fat-free chicken broth
1½ cups finely chopped fresh broccoli
¼ teaspoon salt
⅛ teaspoon pepper
1½ cups (6 ounces) shredded reduced-fat sharp cheddar cheese

1. Coat a large saucepan with cooking spray, and place over medium heat until hot. Add onion; sauté 5 minutes. Add potato, milk, and broth; bring to a boil. Partially cover, reduce heat, and simmer 25 minutes. Remove 1 cup potato mixture, and set aside. Place remaining potato mixture in a blender, and process until smooth.

2. Return potato purée to pan; stir in broccoli, salt, and pepper. Partially cover, and cook over medium heat 8 minutes, stirring frequently. Add reserved potato mixture; cook 1 minute. Remove from heat; add cheese, stirring until cheese melts. Yield: 6 servings (serving size: 1 cup).

POINTS: 4; **Exchanges:** 1½ Starch, 1 Med-fat Meat
Per serving: CAL 209 (27% from fat); PRO 13.4g; FAT 6.2g (sat 3.6g); CARB 25.2g; FIB 2.7g; CHOL 21mg; IRON 1.1mg; SOD 347mg; CALC 350mg

Prosciutto-and-Fontina Panini

1 (5.25-ounce) package focaccia (Italian flatbread) or 1 (8-ounce) package Italian cheese-flavored pizza crust (such as Boboli)
8 very thin slices prosciutto (about 2 ounces)
¼ cup (1 ounce) shredded fontina cheese
1 cup trimmed arugula or watercress
2 (⅛-inch-thick) red onion slices, separated into rings
2 teaspoons balsamic vinegar
⅛ teaspoon pepper

1. Preheat oven to 300°.

2. Slice each bread round in half horizontally. Divide prosciutto slices evenly between bottom halves of bread; top each bread half with fontina cheese, arugula, and red onion slices. Drizzle balsamic vinegar over sandwiches, and sprinkle with pepper; cover with top halves of bread. Wrap sandwiches tightly in aluminum foil; bake at 300° for 15 minutes. Yield: 2 servings.

POINTS: 7; **Exchanges:** 2½ Starch, 1½ Med-fat Meat, 1 Veg
Per serving: CAL 330 (31% from fat); PRO 20.2g; FAT 11.5g (sat 5.6g); CARB 40.3g; FIB 4.3g; CHOL 33mg; IRON 0.9mg; SOD 846mg; CALC 220mg

Garlic Gazpacho

2¼ pounds plum tomatoes, halved
1   cup coarsely chopped yellow bell
    pepper
1   cup peeled seeded cucumber, coarsely
    chopped
¼   cup sherry vinegar
1   teaspoon olive oil
½   teaspoon salt
½   teaspoon black pepper
⅛   to ¼ teaspoon ground red pepper
6   garlic cloves
4   ice cubes

1. Place all ingredients in a food processor or blender, and process until smooth. Pour into a large bowl; cover and chill. Yield: 6 servings (serving size: 1 cup).

POINTS: 1; **Exchanges:** 2 Veg
Per serving: CAL 67 (20% from fat); PRO 2g; FAT 1.5g (sat 0.2g); CARB 11.5g; FIB 2.8g; CHOL 0mg; IRON 1.3mg; SOD 272mg; CALC 22mg

Turkey-Vegetable Sloppy Joes

1   pound ground turkey
1   cup chopped onion
1   garlic clove, minced
½   cup chopped green bell pepper
1   (14.5-ounce) can diced tomatoes
¼   cup tomato paste
1   tablespoon yellow mustard
1   teaspoon chili powder
¾   teaspoon ground cumin
½   teaspoon salt
½   teaspoon pepper
4   (2-ounce) kaiser rolls or hamburger buns,
    split
1   cup (4 ounces) shredded reduced-fat sharp
    cheddar cheese

1. Cook turkey, onion, and garlic in a nonstick skillet over medium-high heat until turkey is browned, stirring to crumble. Stir in bell pepper and next 7 ingredients. Bring to a boil; cover. Reduce heat; simmer 10 minutes, stirring occasionally.

Add a glass of wine to this Prosciutto-and-Fontina Panini and you're supping alfresco on the Piazza San Marco.

French Onion Burger

2. Spoon ½ cup turkey mixture onto bottom half of each roll; top each with 2 tablespoons cheese and top half of roll. Yield: 8 servings.

POINTS: 5; Exchanges: 1½ Starch, 1½ Lean Meat, ½ Med-fat Meat
Per serving: CAL 232 (25% from fat); PRO 20.8g; FAT 6.4g (sat 2.5g); CARB 22.8g; FIB 1.4g; CHOL 46mg; IRON 3mg; SOD 576mg; CALC 170mg

French Onion Burgers

2 teaspoons vegetable oil
2 cups chopped onion
1 pound ground round
¼ teaspoon pepper
1 large egg white, lightly beaten
1 teaspoon salt
4 (1½-ounce) French bread rolls or hamburger buns, split and toasted
4 teaspoons fat-free French or blue cheese dressing

1. Heat oil in a 12-inch cast-iron skillet over medium-high heat. Add onion; sauté 10 minutes or until tender. Spoon onion into a bowl; let cool.

2. Add beef, pepper, and egg white to onion; stir well. Divide beef mixture into 4 equal portions, shaping into ¾-inch-thick patties.

3. Sprinkle salt evenly over surface of skillet. Heat salt in skillet over high heat 2 minutes. Add patties; cook 5 minutes on each side or until done. Place patties on bottom halves of rolls; top each with 1 teaspoon dressing and top halves of buns. Yield: 4 servings.

POINTS: 7; Exchanges: 2 Starch, 3½ Lean Meat
Per serving: CAL 340 (21% from fat); PRO 31.6g; FAT 7.8g (sat 2.4g); CARB 33.1g; FIB 2.3g; CHOL 66mg; IRON 3.5mg; SOD 957mg; CALC 40mg

Eggplant-and-Feta Pitas

16 (½-inch-thick) slices eggplant
Cooking spray
4 (6-inch) pita bread rounds, cut in half
8 (½-inch-thick) slices tomato
¼ cup (1 ounce) crumbled feta cheese with peppercorns
¼ cup chopped red onion
12 large fresh basil leaves, thinly sliced

1. Preheat oven to 425°.

2. Arrange eggplant in a single layer in a 13- x 9-

inch baking dish coated with cooking spray. Cover and bake at 425° for 10 minutes. Turn eggplant over, and cook, uncovered, 10 minutes. Let cool slightly.

3. Fill each pita half with 2 eggplant slices, 1 tomato slice, 1½ teaspoons cheese, 1½ teaspoons onion, and basil leaves. Yield: 4 servings.

POINTS: 3; Exchanges: 2 Starch, 1 Veg
Per serving: CAL 190 (17% from fat); PRO 7.2g; FAT 3.5g (sat 1.4g); CARB 34.2g; FIB 4g; CHOL 6mg; IRON 2.1mg; SOD 311mg; CALC 118mg

Turkey-Havarti Grinder

⅓ cup mango chutney
2 tablespoons chopped unsalted, dry-roasted peanuts
2 tablespoons light mayonnaise
Dash of ground red pepper
1 (16-ounce) loaf French bread
1 pound very thinly sliced deli turkey breast
6 curly leaf lettuce leaves
2 ounces thinly sliced reduced-fat Havarti cheese
6 sandwich-cut bread-and-butter pickles
1 medium Red Delicious apple, cored and sliced into rings

1. Combine first 4 ingredients; stir well. Cut bread loaf in half horizontally, and spread chutney mixture over bottom half of bread; top with turkey, lettuce, cheese, pickles, apple, and top half of bread. Cut loaf into 8 pieces. Yield: 8 servings.

POINTS: 6; Exchanges: 3 Starch, 1½ Very Lean Meat, ½ Fat
Per serving: CAL 321 (17% from fat); PRO 19.1g; FAT 5.9g (sat 1.3g); CARB 45g; FIB 2.3g; CHOL 8mg; IRON 1.8mg; SOD 951mg; CALC 94mg

Garden Grilled Cheese

Our Test Kitchens found that it works well to flatten the sandwiches as they cook by placing another skillet on top of them.

8 teaspoons Dijon mustard
8 (1-ounce) slices sourdough bread
1 cup (4 ounces) shredded reduced-fat sharp cheddar cheese
½ cup drained canned artichoke hearts, sliced
1⅓ cups sliced bottled roasted red bell peppers
Cooking spray

1. Spread 2 teaspoons mustard on each of 4 bread slices; top each with ¼ cup cheese, 2 tablespoons artichoke, ⅓ cup bell peppers, and 1 bread slice.

2. Coat a large nonstick skillet with cooking spray; place over medium heat until hot. Add sandwiches to skillet; cook 2 minutes on each side or until golden brown. Yield: 4 servings.

POINTS: 6; **Exchanges:** 2½ Starch, 1 Med-fat Meat
Per serving: CAL 264 (26% from fat); PRO 14.8g; FAT 7.6g (sat 3.2g); CARB 34.7g; FIB 0.9g; CHOL 19mg; IRON 2.9mg; SOD 951mg; CALC 321mg

Smoked Turkey-and-Watercress Pitas

¼ cup plain fat-free yogurt
2 tablespoons spicy hot mustard
2 (6-inch) pita bread rounds, cut in half
4 (1-ounce) slices smoked deli turkey breast
8 (¼-inch-thick) slices tomato
1 cup trimmed watercress
½ cup (2 ounces) shredded reduced-fat, reduced-sodium Swiss cheese

1. Combine yogurt and mustard in a small bowl; stir well. Spread mustard sauce evenly on inside surface of each pita half. Place 1 turkey slice, 2 tomato slices, and ¼ cup watercress in each half; sprinkle each with 2 tablespoons cheese. Yield: 4 servings.

POINTS: 4; **Exchanges:** 1 Starch, 1 Very Lean Meat, ½ Med-fat Meat
Per serving: CAL 166 (30% from fat); PRO 15.2g; FAT 5.5g (sat 2.2g); CARB 14.3g; FIB 1.1g; CHOL 26mg; IRON 1.5mg; SOD 415mg; CALC 225mg

Spinach makes a fine substitution for watercress in Smoked Turkey-and-Watercress Pitas.

Creamy Lentil Soup

Cooking spray
1 tablespoon olive oil
1 cup sliced carrot
1 cup chopped onion
2 (14¼-ounce) cans fat-free chicken broth
1 (8-ounce) can no-salt-added tomato sauce
2 cups water
1 cup dried lentils
⅓ cup uncooked long-grain rice
½ teaspoon salt
½ teaspoon ground cumin
½ teaspoon coarsely ground pepper
2 cups 2% reduced-fat milk

1. Coat a large Dutch oven with cooking spray; add oil, and place over medium-high heat until hot. Add carrot and onion; sauté 5 minutes or until tender. Stir in broth and next 7 ingredients; bring to a boil. Cover, reduce heat, and simmer 45 minutes or until lentils are tender.

2. Place half of lentil mixture in a food processor; process until smooth. Pour purée into a bowl. Repeat procedure with remaining lentil mixture. Return purée to pan. Stir in milk; cook over low heat until thoroughly heated. Yield: 6 servings (serving size: 1½ cups).

POINTS: 4; **Exchanges:** 2½ Starch, ½ Fat, 1 Very Lean Meat
Per serving: CAL 252 (16% from fat); PRO 13.6g; FAT 4.4g (sat 1.4g); CARB 38.9g; FIB 4.9g; CHOL 7mg; IRON 3.7mg; SOD 258mg; CALC 133mg

French Onion Soup Gratiné

Make this soup in a large casserole so it won't overflow.

2 cups thinly sliced onion, separated into rings
1½ teaspoons olive oil
¼ teaspoon sugar
1½ cups water
1 cup dry red wine
¼ teaspoon pepper
1 (10½-ounce) can beef broth
4 (½-ounce) slices diagonally cut French bread, toasted
½ cup (2 ounces) shredded reduced-fat, reduced-sodium Swiss cheese

1. Combine first 3 ingredients in a 3-quart casserole; stir well. Cover and microwave at HIGH 12

to 14 minutes or until onion is tender, stirring after 6 minutes. Add water, wine, pepper, and broth; cover and microwave at HIGH 10 minutes, stirring after 5 minutes. Spoon 1 cup soup into each of 4 microwave-safe bowls, and top each with 1 bread slice and 2 tablespoons cheese. Microwave at HIGH for 1 minute or until cheese melts. Yield: 4 servings.

POINTS: 3; **Exchanges:** 1 Starch, 1 Med-fat Meat
Per serving: CAL 154 (31% from fat); PRO 9.4g; FAT 5.3g (sat 2.4g); CARB 17.4g; FIB 1.4g; CHOL 25mg; IRON 1.1mg; SOD 605mg; CALC 174mg

New England Fish Chowder

2   tablespoons margarine
3   tablespoons shredded carrot
2   tablespoons diced celery
2   tablespoons minced fresh onion
2   tablespoons plus 1 teaspoon all-purpose flour
3½ cups skim milk, divided
2   cups peeled diced baking potato
½   teaspoon salt
¼   teaspoon pepper
1   pound cod or other lean white fish fillets, cut into 1-inch pieces
Unsalted oyster crackers (optional)

1. Melt margarine in a medium saucepan over medium heat. Add carrot, celery, and onion; sauté 2 minutes. Stir in flour. Gradually add 2½ cups skim milk, stirring constantly with a whisk. Add potato, salt, and pepper; bring to a boil. Reduce heat, and simmer, uncovered, 30 minutes, stirring occasionally. Add fish and remaining 1 cup skim milk; cook an additional 10 minutes or until fish is done. Serve chowder with oyster crackers, if desired. Yield: 4 servings (serving size: 1½ cups).

POINTS: 6; **Exchanges:** 2 Starch, 3 Very Lean Meat, 1 Fat
Per serving: CAL 299 (21% from fat); PRO 29.6g; FAT 6.9g (sat 1.5g); CARB 28.3g; FIB 1.6g; CHOL 53mg; IRON 1.3mg; SOD 541mg; CALC 297mg

New England Fish Chowder oozes with creamy, hearty flavor—in less than an hour.

Roast-and-Relish Sandwiches look and taste like a deli hero—without the fat.

Roast-and-Relish Sandwiches

A chow-chow-spiked cabbage mixture nestles under mounds of roast beef in these hefty sandwiches.

½ cup chopped red cabbage
¼ cup finely chopped green onions
¼ cup chow-chow
2 (3-ounce) whole-wheat submarine rolls, split
4 ounces thinly sliced cooked lean roast beef

1. Combine first 3 ingredients; spoon evenly over bottom halves of rolls. Top evenly with roast beef, and cover with roll tops. Yield: 2 servings.

POINTS: 8; **Exchanges:** 4 Starch, 2 Lean Meat
Per serving: CAL 426 (16% from fat); PRO 27.5g; FAT 7.6g (sat 1.3g); CARB 61.5g; FIB 3.6g; CHOL 48mg; IRON 4.1mg; SOD 738mg; CALC 128mg

Cauliflower Vichyssoise

1 teaspoon margarine
1 cup chopped leek
1 garlic clove, crushed
1¾ cups chopped cauliflower
1 cup peeled diced red potato
1 cup water
¼ teaspoon salt
⅛ teaspoon ground nutmeg
2 (10½-ounce) cans low-salt chicken broth
¾ cup evaporated skim milk
Freshly ground pepper (optional)

1. Melt margarine in a saucepan over medium heat. Add leek and garlic; sauté 4 minutes. Add cauliflower and next 5 ingredients; bring to a boil. Reduce heat; simmer, uncovered, 30 minutes or until vegetables are tender, stirring occasionally.
2. Place half of cauliflower mixture in a blender, and process until smooth. Pour into a bowl, and repeat procedure with remaining cauliflower mixture. Stir in milk. Cover and chill. Serve with freshly ground pepper, if desired. Yield: 5 cups (serving size: 1 cup).

POINTS: 2; **Exchanges:** 1 Starch, 1 Veg
Per serving: CAL 118 (14% from fat); PRO 6.6g; FAT 1.9g (sat 0.6g); CARB 20.1g; FIB 2.4g; CHOL 2mg; IRON 1.9mg; SOD 226mg; CALC 148mg

Fresh Peach Soup

3   cups diced honeydew melon
½   cup fresh orange juice
½   cup vanilla low-fat yogurt
1   tablespoon honey
2   teaspoons fresh lime juice
1   teaspoon peeled finely chopped fresh
    ginger
2   cups peeled diced peaches (about 1½
    pounds)
1   cup blueberries

1. Place first 6 ingredients in a blender; process until mixture is smooth. Combine melon mixture, diced peaches, and blueberries in a large bowl; stir well. Cover and chill. Yield: 6 servings (serving size: 1 cup).

POINTS: 2; **Exchanges:** 1½ Fruit
Per serving: CAL 107 (4% from fat); PRO 2.1g; FAT 0.5g (sat 0.2g); CARB 26g; FIB 2.9g; CHOL 1mg; IRON 0.2mg; SOD 23mg; CALC 44mg

Tangy Grouper Sandwiches

You'll think you're at the beach when you bite into this mammoth seafood sandwich. The homemade tartar sauce lends just the right sweet and salty sensations to the tender grilled fish.

2   tablespoons lemon juice
1   teaspoon low-sodium Worcestershire
    sauce
1   teaspoon olive oil
½   teaspoon pepper
⅛   teaspoon paprika
3   tablespoons nonfat mayonnaise
1   tablespoon minced onion
2   teaspoons dill pickle relish
½   teaspoon yellow mustard
1   (1-pound) grouper fillet, cut into
    4 pieces
Cooking spray
4   green leaf lettuce leaves
12 (¼-inch-thick) slices Roma tomato
4   hamburger buns, split and toasted

1. Combine first 5 ingredients; set aside. Combine mayonnaise, onion, pickle relish, and mustard; set aside.

2. Prepare grill. Place fish on grill rack coated with cooking spray; grill, covered, 5 minutes on each side or until fish flakes when tested with a fork, basting with lemon juice mixture.

3. Layer 1 lettuce leaf, 3 slices tomato, and 1 piece fish on bottom half of each bun. Spoon mayonnaise mixture over fish; cover with top halves of buns. Serve immediately. Yield: 4 servings.

POINTS: 5; **Exchanges:** 1½ Starch, 3 Very Lean Meat
Per serving: CAL 243 (20% from fat); PRO 25g; FAT 5.3g (sat 0.8g); CARB 22.6g; FIB 1g; CHOL 52mg; IRON 3mg; SOD 338mg; CALC 90mg

Shrimp-Tortellini Soup

1   (9-ounce) package fresh cheese tortellini
3   cups broccoli florets
4   teaspoons olive oil
1   pound medium shrimp, peeled and
    deveined
1½ cups sliced crimini or white mushrooms
¼   cup chopped red onion
2   (14¼-ounce) cans fat-free chicken
    broth
1   teaspoon ground ginger
½   teaspoon salt
Red onion slices, separated into rings
    (optional)

1. Bring 4 quarts water to a boil in a large Dutch oven. Add cheese tortellini, and cook 4 minutes. Add broccoli, and cook an additional 5 minutes or until tortellini is tender. Drain in a colander, and set aside.

2. Heat olive oil in pan over medium-high heat. Add shrimp, sliced mushrooms, and chopped onion; sauté 3 minutes or until shrimp is done.

Any firm, white-fleshed fish can be substituted in Tangy Grouper Sandwiches.

¼ teaspoon garlic powder
¼ teaspoon ground allspice
¼ teaspoon pepper
1 bay leaf

1. Trim fat from leg of lamb, and cut lamb into 1-inch cubes.

2. Coat a Dutch oven with cooking spray, and place over medium-high heat until hot. Add lamb cubes, and cook 5 minutes or until browned. Add cabbage and remaining ingredients; bring to a boil. Cover, reduce heat, and simmer 20 minutes or until lamb is tender, stirring occasionally. Discard bay leaf. Yield: 4 servings (serving size: 2 cups).

POINTS: 6; **Exchanges:** 4 Lean Meat, 2 Veg, 1 Starch
Per serving: CAL 331 (18% from fat); PRO 38.6g; FAT 7g (sat 2.4g); CARB 27.9g; FIB 5.8g; CHOL 119mg; IRON 4.7mg; SOD 1,084mg; CALC 70mg

Linda's Quick Bean Soup

6 cups chopped fresh kale (about ¾ pound)
1 cup chopped onion
1 teaspoon garlic powder
1 teaspoon onion powder
3 (16-ounce) cans kidney beans, undrained
2 (14½-ounce) cans no-salt-added whole tomatoes, undrained and chopped
1 (15-ounce) can chickpeas (garbanzo beans), undrained
1 (14¼-ounce) can fat-free chicken broth

1. Combine all ingredients in a large Dutch oven, and bring mixture to a boil. Cover, reduce heat, and simmer 1 hour. Yield: 13 servings (serving size: 1 cup).

POINTS: 3; **Exchanges:** 1 Starch, 1 Veg, 1 Very Lean Meat
Per serving: CAL 210 (6% from fat); PRO 12.9g; FAT 1.3g (sat 0.2g); CARB 38.6g; FIB 4.9g; CHOL 0mg; IRON 4.3mg; SOD 438mg; CALC 102mg

Potato-Corn Chowder

You can bet the folks on our foods staff will be stirring up this chunky vegetable chowder in their own kitchens this winter. They lined up to make copies of the recipe after taste testing.

Lamb-and-Barley Soup is loaded with chunky vegetables.

Add chicken broth, ginger, and salt; bring to a boil. Add tortellini mixture, and cook until thoroughly heated. Ladle soup into bowls, and garnish with onion rings, if desired. Yield: 4 servings (serving size: 2 cups).

POINTS: 9; **Exchanges:** 2½ Starch, 1 Veg, 1 Fat, 4 Very Lean Meat, ½ Med-fat Meat
Per serving: CAL 430 (24% from fat); PRO 42.5g; FAT 11.5g (sat 3g); CARB 40.2g; FIB 4.4g; CHOL 199mg; IRON 4.1mg; SOD 880mg; CALC 117mg

Lamb-and-Barley Soup

1¼ pounds lean boned leg of lamb, cut into 1-inch cubes
Cooking spray
2 cups coarsely chopped green cabbage
2 (10½-ounce) cans beef broth
1 cup water
1 cup chopped carrot
1 cup chopped onion
1 cup peeled chopped rutabaga
⅓ cup uncooked quick-cooking barley
1 teaspoon dried thyme

Cooking spray
¾ cup chopped green pepper
⅓ cup chopped onion
2¾ cup canned reduced-sodium chicken broth, undiluted
2 cups chopped red potato
1 teaspoon salt
¼ teaspoon pepper
¼ cup cornstarch
2¼ cups skim milk
2¼ cups frozen whole kernel corn
1 (2-ounce) jar diced pimiento

1. Place a medium saucepan coated with cooking spray over medium-high heat. Add green pepper and onion; cook, stirring constantly, 5 minutes, or until vegetables are tender. Stir in broth and next 3 ingredients. Bring to a boil; reduce heat, and simmer, uncovered, 6 to 8 minutes or until potato is tender.

2. Combine cornstarch and milk, stirring until smooth; gradually add to potato mixture, stirring constantly. Stir in corn and pimiento; bring to a boil over medium heat, stirring constantly. Cook, stirring constantly, 1 minute or until mixture is thickened. Serve immediately. Yield: 5 servings (serving size: 1½ cups).

POINTS: 3; **Exchanges:** 1½ Starch, ½ Sk Milk
Per serving: CAL 167 (5% from fat); PRO 8.4g; FAT 0.9g (sat 0.2g); CARB 33.5g; FIB 2.6g; CHOL 2mg; IRON 1.5mg; SOD 841mg; CALC 150mg

Shrimp Calzones

1 (10-ounce) can refrigerated pizza crust dough
⅓ cup Italian-style tomato paste
1 tablespoon water
¼ teaspoon dried Italian seasoning
1 (8-ounce) package frozen cooked salad shrimp, thawed and drained
Butter-flavored cooking spray
1 tablespoon grated Parmesan cheese

1. Preheat oven to 400°.

2. Roll pizza crust into an 18- x 10-inch rectangle. Cut into 6 (6- x 5-inch) rectangles.

3. Combine tomato paste, water, and Italian seasoning in a bowl; stir well. Spread mixture evenly over dough rectangles, leaving a ½-inch border. Arrange shrimp evenly over half of each rectangle, and brush edges of rectangles with water. Fold rectangles in half to cover shrimp; press edges together with a fork.

4. Place calzones on a large baking sheet coated with cooking spray. Coat tops of calzones with cooking spray; sprinkle evenly with Parmesan cheese. Bake at 400° for 18 minutes or until lightly browned. Yield: 6 servings.

POINTS: 3; **Exchanges:** 1½ Starch, 1½ Very Lean Meat
Per serving: CAL 182 (13% from fat); PRO 12.8g; FAT 2.7g (sat 0.6g); CARB 24.8g; FIB 2.2g; CHOL 74mg; IRON 2mg; SOD 370mg; CALC 57mg

Using prepared dough takes all the fuss out of Shrimp Calzones.

KNOW WHEN TO FOLD 'EM

Literally Italian for "pant leg," calzone is a pizza folded onto itself. From a traditional mozzarella cheese-and-sausage calzone to a gourmet caramelized onion-and-blue cheese version, the calzone is limited only by the ingredients on hand.

But no matter what flavors you prefer, the key to a successful calzone is to avoid making the filling too moist. If moist, the filling creates steam, which in turn makes the dough mushy. Calzones are often served with warm fat-free marinara sauce for dipping. That way, you get the flavor of the sauce with each bite of crispy, golden calzone.

Complements

FOOD IS NOURISHMENT, BUT A MEAL
IS A MASTERPIECE; THESE ARE THE
RECIPES THAT SEPARATE THE TWO.

Zucchini-Lemon Muffins

Cranberry-Kumquat Salsa intensifies in flavor the longer it is stored.

Zucchini-Lemon Muffins

For a light lunch, Zucchini-Lemon Muffins complement chicken salad.

2   cups all-purpose flour
½   cup sugar
1   tablespoon baking powder
2   teaspoons grated lemon rind
¼   teaspoon salt
¼   teaspoon ground nutmeg
1   cup shredded zucchini
¾   cup skim milk
3   tablespoons vegetable oil
1   large egg
Cooking spray

1. Preheat oven to 400°.

2. Combine flour, sugar, baking powder, lemon rind, salt, and nutmeg in a bowl; make a well in center of mixture. Combine zucchini, milk, oil, and egg; stir well. Add to dry ingredients, stirring just until moist.

3. Divide batter evenly among 12 muffin cups coated with cooking spray. Bake at 400° for 20 minutes or until golden. Remove muffins from pan immediately; let cool on a wire rack. Yield: 12 muffins (serving size: 1 muffin).

POINTS: 3; **Exchanges:** 1½ Starch, ½ Fat
Per serving: CAL 147 (26% from fat); PRO 3.1g; FAT 4.3g (sat 0.8g); CARB 24.3g; FIB 0.6g; CHOL 18mg; IRON 1.1mg; SOD 62mg; CALC 69mg

Cranberry-Kumquat Salsa

2   cups fresh or frozen cranberries
6   kumquats, unpeeled and coarsely chopped
3   tablespoons minced crystallized ginger
2   jalapeño peppers, seeded and finely chopped
¾   cup sugar
¼   cup minced fresh mint

1. Position knife blade in food processor bowl; drop cranberries through food chute with processor running, and process 15 seconds or until minced. Transfer cranberries to a small bowl.

2. Position knife blade in processor bowl; add kumquats, ginger, and peppers. Pulse 3 to 5 times or until mixture is finely chopped.

3. Add kumquat mixture to cranberries. Stir in sugar and mint. Cover and store in refrigerator.

Flavor intensifies the longer salsa is chilled. Serve with chicken, pork, or turkey or as a spread over nonfat cream cheese; or stir into low-fat yogurt. Yield: 1¾ cups (serving size: 1 tablespoon).

POINTS: 1; **Exchanges:** ½ Fruit
Per serving: CAL 30 (0% from fat); PRO 0.1g; FAT 0g (sat 0g); CARB 7.7g; FIB 0.2g; CHOL 0mg; IRON 0.3mg; SOD 1mg; CALC 5mg

Buttermilk Corn Muffins

1   cup yellow cornmeal
1   cup all-purpose flour
1   tablespoon sugar
2   teaspoons baking powder
½   teaspoon salt
¼   teaspoon baking soda
1½ cups fat-free buttermilk
3   tablespoons vegetable oil
2   large egg whites, lightly beaten
Cooking spray

1. Preheat oven to 425°.

2. Combine first 6 ingredients in a bowl; make a well in center of mixture. Combine buttermilk, oil, and egg whites in a bowl; stir well. Add to dry ingredients, stirring just until moist.

3. Divide batter evenly among 15 muffin cups coated with cooking spray. Bake at 425° for 12 minutes or until golden. Remove muffins from pans immediately. Yield: 15 muffins (serving size: 1 muffin).

POINTS: 2; **Exchanges:** 1 Starch, ½ Fat
Per serving: CAL 105 (28% from fat); PRO 3g; FAT 3.3g (sat 0.6g); CARB 15.7g; FIB 0.7g; CHOL 1mg; IRON 0.8mg; SOD 165mg; CALC 54mg

Lemon-Poppy Seed Muffins

1¾ cups all-purpose flour
½   cup sugar
5   teaspoons poppy seeds
2   teaspoons baking powder
¼   teaspoon salt
1   cup skim milk
3   tablespoons vegetable oil
1   tablespoon grated lemon rind
1   tablespoon fresh lemon juice
1   large egg, lightly beaten
Cooking spray

1. Preheat oven to 400°.

2. Combine first 5 ingredients in a large bowl; make a well in the center of mixture. Combine milk and next 4 ingredients in a bowl; stir well. Add milk mixture to dry ingredients, stirring just until moist.

3. Divide batter evenly among 12 muffin cups coated with cooking spray. Bake at 400° for 25 minutes or until golden. Remove muffins from pans immediately; let cool on a wire rack. Yield: 12 muffins (serving size: 1 muffin).

POINTS: 3; **Exchanges:** 1½ Starch, ½ Fat
Per serving: CAL 146 (30% from fat); PRO 3.2g; FAT 4.8g (sat 0.9g); CARB 22.8g; FIB 0.5g; CHOL 18mg; IRON 1.8mg; SOD 116mg; CALC 78mg

Cranberry Sangría

Get the full-bodied flavor of an authentic sangría with just four ingredients.

1   (48-ounce) bottle cranberry juice
    cocktail
3   cups port or other sweet red wine
1   navel orange, thinly sliced
1   lemon, thinly sliced

1. Combine all ingredients in a large pitcher; cover and chill at least 3 hours. Yield: 10 cups (serving size: 1 cup).

POINTS: 4; **Exchanges:** 2½ Starch
Per serving: CAL 202 (0% from fat); PRO 0.4g; FAT 0.1g (sat 0g); CARB 31.7g; FIB 0.6g; CHOL 0mg; IRON 0.6mg; SOD 9mg; CALC 19mg

Santa Fe Salsa

Once you taste the freshness of this salsa, it'll be hard to go back to bottled.

1   cup finely chopped tomato
½   cup finely chopped red onion
⅛   teaspoon salt
1   (4-ounce) can chopped green chiles,
    undrained
1   large garlic clove, minced

1. Combine all ingredients in a small bowl; stir well. Cover and chill at least 2 hours. Serve with chicken or beef or as a dip with baked tortilla chips. Yield: 1¾ cups (serving size: ¼ cup).

POINTS: 0; **Exchanges:** Free
Per serving: CAL 14 (6% from fat); PRO 0.5g; FAT 0.1g (sat 0g); CARB 3.2g; FIB 0.7g; CHOL 0mg; IRON 0.2mg; SOD 43mg; CALC 5mg

Peach Champagne Slush

4½ cups peeled sliced fresh peaches (about 2 pounds)
1   cup pink champagne
⅓   cup sifted powdered sugar

1. Combine all ingredients in a blender; process until smooth. Pour into a shallow baking dish; cover and freeze at least 3 hours. Let stand at room temperature for 30 minutes or until slushy. Serve immediately. Yield: 5 cups (serving size: ½ cup).

POINTS: 1; **Exchanges:** ½ Fruit, ½ Starch
Per serving: CAL 66 (1% from fat); PRO 0.6g; FAT 0.1g (sat 0g); CARB 12.7g; FIB 1.2g; CHOL 0mg; IRON 0.2mg; SOD 1mg; CALC 5mg

Papaya Seed Dressing

The next time you buy fresh papayas, don't throw away the seeds. Their peppery flavor adds mysterious pungency to this salad dressing.

1   tablespoon cornstarch
1   (7.1-ounce) can papaya nectar
½   cup sugar
½   cup white wine vinegar
3   tablespoons fresh papaya seeds (about 1 papaya)
2   tablespoons chopped onion
½   teaspoon salt
½   teaspoon dry mustard

1. Combine cornstarch and papaya nectar in a small saucepan; stir with a whisk until blended. Bring to a boil over medium heat, and cook 1 minute or until thick, stirring constantly. Pour mixture into a medium bowl; let cool.

2. Combine sugar and next 5 ingredients in a blender; process until papaya seeds resemble coarsely ground pepper. Add to nectar mixture; stir well. Cover and chill at least 2 hours. Serve over mixed fruit. Yield 2 cups (serving size: 2 tablespoons).

POINTS: 1; **Exchanges:** ½ Fruit
Per serving: CAL 36 (3% from fat); PRO 0.1g; FAT 0.1g (sat 0g); CARB 9.4g; FIB 0.1g; CHOL 0mg; IRON 0.1mg; SOD 74mg; CALC 3mg

Watermelon Daiquiri

4   cups peeled, seeded, and cubed watermelon
½   cup white rum
¼   cup fresh lime juice
¼   cup triple sec (orange-flavored liqueur)
Ice cubes

1. Freeze watermelon cubes in a shallow pan at least 6 hours.

2. Combine frozen watermelon, rum, lime juice, and liqueur in a blender; process until smooth. Add enough ice to bring mixture to 5-cup level on blender container; process until smooth. Yield: 5 cups (serving size: 1 cup).

POINTS: 3; **Exchanges:** 1 Fruit, 1 Starch
Per serving: CAL 136 (4% from fat); PRO 0.8g; FAT 0.6g (sat 0.3g); CARB 13.6g; FIB 0.7g; CHOL 0mg; IRON 0.2mg; SOD 3mg; CALC 11mg

Blue Cheese Spread

1   (8-ounce) block fat-free cream cheese, softened
¼   cup (1 ounce) crumbled blue cheese
2   tablespoons finely chopped onion
1   tablespoon skim milk
1   tablespoon reduced-sodium Worcestershire sauce

1. Combine all ingredients in a bowl, and stir well. Serve with French bread or crackers or as a sandwich spread. Yield: 1¼ cups (serving size: 1 tablespoon).

POINTS: 0; **Exchanges:** Free
Per serving: CAL 16 (23% from fat); PRO 2g; FAT 0.4g (sat 0.3g); CARB 1.1g; FIB 0g; CHOL 3mg; IRON 0mg; SOD 78mg; CALC 41mg

Raisin-Nut Spread

4   ounces light cream cheese, softened (about ½ cup)
3   tablespoons honey
¼   teaspoon ground cinnamon
3   tablespoons chopped pecans
3   tablespoons chopped raisins

1. Combine cream cheese, honey, and cinnamon in a bowl; stir well. Add pecans and raisins, and stir well. Serve with bagels, English muffins, waffles, or pancakes. Yield: ¾ cup (serving size: 1 tablespoon).

POINTS: 1; **Exchanges:** ½ Fat, ½ Starch
Per serving: CAL 56 (47% from fat); PRO 1.2g; FAT 2.9g (sat 1.1g); CARB 7.1g; FIB 0.3g; CHOL 5mg; IRON 0.1mg; SOD 54mg; CALC 15mg

Peach Champagne Slush and
Lemon Cookies (page 93)

Spoon Melon-Jalapeño Salsa over grilled fish, shrimp, or pork for an easy summer entrée.

Melon-Jalapeño Salsa

You don't have to buy three whole melons to make this salsa. Larger grocery stores sell fresh melon cubes in the produce department so you can buy smaller amounts. This saves prep time too.

1   cup peeled, seeded, and cubed honeydew melon
1   cup peeled, seeded, and cubed cantaloupe
1   cup peeled, seeded, and cubed watermelon
1   red jalapeño pepper, seeded and finely chopped
1   green jalapeño pepper, seeded and finely chopped
2   tablespoons fresh lime juice
¼   cup finely chopped fresh basil

1. Combine all ingredients in a bowl; stir well. Cover and chill at least 3 hours. Serve with grilled fish, shrimp, chicken, or pork. Yield: 3 cups (serving size: ¼ cup).

Note: Use 2 green jalapeño peppers if red jalapeños are not available.

POINTS: 0; **Exchanges:** Free
Per serving: CAL 15 (6% from fat); PRO 0.3g; FAT 0.1g (sat 0.1g); CARB 3.8g; FIB 0.4g; CHOL 0mg; IRON 0.1mg; SOD 3mg; CALC 5mg

Jalapeño Jelly

We've skipped the canning process to make an easy, small-batch, keep-in-the-fridge jelly. It's a cool appetizer (or relish) with just a little heat.

3   jalapeño peppers, seeded and coarsely chopped
½   green bell pepper, coarsely chopped
3   cups sugar
½   cup cider vinegar
½   (6-ounce) package liquid fruit pectin
2   tablespoons fresh lime juice

1. Place jalapeño peppers and bell pepper in a food processor; process until smooth.

2. Combine pepper purée, sugar, and vinegar in a large nonaluminum saucepan. Bring to a boil over medium-high heat, and cook 3 minutes, stirring constantly. Stir in pectin and lime juice; cook 1 minute, stirring constantly. Remove from heat, and skim off foam with a metal spoon.

3. Pour evenly into 3 hot, sterilized half-pint jars, filling each to within ¼ inch of top; wipe jar rims. Cover immediately with metal lids, and screw on bands. Let cool.

4. Store in refrigerator. Serve over fat-free cream cheese with crackers or toast as an appetizer or with meats as a relish. Yield: 3 half-pints (serving size: 1 tablespoon).

POINTS: 1; **Exchanges:** ½ Starch
Per serving: CAL 49 (0% from fat); PRO 0g; FAT 0g (sat 0g); CARB 12.8g; FIB 0g; CHOL 0mg; IRON 0mg; SOD 0mg; CALC 0mg

Basil-Parsley Pesto

2 tablespoons pine nuts
4 garlic cloves
1½ cups fresh basil leaves
½ cup chopped fresh parsley
⅓ cup (1⅓ ounce) grated fresh Parmesan cheese
½ cup fat-free Italian dressing

1. Drop pine nuts and garlic through food chute with food processor on; process 5 seconds or until garlic is minced. Add basil and parsley; process 10 seconds or until minced. Add cheese; process until blended. With food processor on, slowly pour Italian dressing through food chute; process until smooth. Spread on chicken or fish before cooking, use as a stuffing for mushroom caps, spread on fresh tomato or baguette slices, or serve on hot pasta. Yield: 1 cup (serving size: 1 tablespoon).

POINTS: 1; **Exchanges:** ½ Fat
Per serving: CAL 22 (61% from fat); PRO 1g; FAT 1.5g (sat 0.4g); CARB 1.7g; FIB 0.1g; CHOL 1mg; IRON 0.1mg; SOD 101mg; CALC 31mg

Strawberry Spread

4 ounces light cream cheese, softened (about ½ cup)
¼ cup strawberry preserves

1. Combine cream cheese and preserves in a bowl; stir well. Serve with bagels, English muffins, waffles, or pancakes. Yield: ¾ cup (serving size: 1 tablespoon).

POINTS: 1; **Exchanges:** ½ Starch
Per serving: CAL 39 (37% from fat); PRO 1g; FAT 1.6g (sat 1g); CARB 5.3g; FIB 0.1g; CHOL 5mg; IRON 0.1mg; SOD 54mg; CALC 14mg

Spicy Barbecue Sauce

In the time it takes to heat the grill, you can prepare this barbecue sauce.

1 (8-ounce) can no-salt-added tomato sauce
½ cup reduced-calorie ketchup
¼ cup red wine vinegar
¼ cup low-sodium Worcestershire sauce
2 tablespoons grated fresh onion
1 tablespoon dark brown sugar
1 tablespoon barbecue smoked seasoning (such as Hickory Liquid Smoke)
1 teaspoon chili powder
1 teaspoon pepper
1 garlic clove, minced
1 bay leaf

1. Combine all ingredients in a medium saucepan; stir well. Bring to a boil over medium heat, stirring frequently. Reduce heat and simmer

Basil-Parsley Pesto blends two herbs in this classic sauce from Genoa, Italy.

PESTO POINTERS

Pesto is an uncooked Italian herb sauce that incorporates fresh basil or a combination of herbs with garlic, pine nuts, olive oil, and Parmesan cheese.

One of the great joys of pesto is that it's so easy to prepare. Traditional Italian cooks make it with a mortar and pestle, preferring the finely minced texture that results. (The word "pesto" comes from the Italian verb *pestare*, meaning to pound or grind.)

Although there's nothing in the world quite like fresh pesto, it can be frozen. Try freezing the sauce in ice cube trays and then refreezing the individual cubes in airtight plastic bags. That way you can have a pungent shot of summer any time of the year or whenever you need a reminder of just how big-hearted Mother Nature can be.

10 minutes, stirring occasionally. Discard bay leaf. Use on pork or poultry. Yield: 2 cups (serving size: 1 tablespoon).

POINTS: 0; **Exchanges:** Free
Per serving: CAL 8 (0% from fat); PRO 0.1g; FAT 0g (sat 0g); CARB 1.8g; FIB 0.2g; CHOL 0mg; IRON 0.1mg; SOD 10mg; CALC 1mg

Roasted Garlic-Lemon Sauce

Looking for a simple entrée with great flavor? Just spoon this sauce over plain grilled chicken or pork.

3   large garlic heads
2   tablespoons fresh lemon juice
1   tablespoon low-sodium soy sauce
1½ teaspoons white wine vinegar
⅛   teaspoon salt
⅛   teaspoon freshly ground pepper

1. Preheat oven to 350°.
2. Remove white papery skin from garlic heads (do not peel or separate the cloves). Cut off top one-third of each garlic head. Wrap each head separately in foil. Bake at 350° for 1 hour; let cool 10 minutes. Squeeze each garlic head to extract garlic pulp. Discard skins.
3. Combine garlic pulp, lemon juice, and remaining ingredients in a small food processor; process until smooth. Serve sauce at room temperature with chicken, pork, or vegetables. Yield: ½ cup (serving size: 1 tablespoon).

POINTS: 1; **Exchanges:** ½ Starch
Per serving: CAL 38 (2% from fat); PRO 1.5g; FAT 0.1g (sat 0g); CARB 8.3g; FIB 0.4g; CHOL 0mg; IRON 0.4mg; SOD 88mg; CALC 44mg

Mint Marinade

Spicy-sweet hoisin sauce, made from soybeans, spices, and chiles, punches up the flavor in this marinade. Use it as a basting sauce or at the table with roasted meat, poultry, or fish.

⅓   cup molasses
¼   cup minced fresh spearmint
1   tablespoon peeled grated fresh ginger
3   tablespoons low-sodium soy sauce
3   tablespoons hoisin sauce
2   tablespoons water
2   garlic cloves, minced

1. Combine all ingredients in a small bowl; stir well. Use immediately or store in refrigerator. Use to marinate beef, pork, or lamb. Yield: ¾ cup (serving size: 1 tablespoon).

POINTS: 1; **Exchanges:** ½ Starch
Per serving: CAL 31 (0% from fat); PRO 0g; FAT 0g (sat 0g); CARB 7.5g; FIB 0g; CHOL 0mg; IRON 0.5mg; SOD 118mg; CALC 20mg

Grapefruit-Cranberry Marmalade

4   medium grapefruit (about 4 pounds)
1½ cups water
2½ cups fresh cranberries
3   cups sugar

1. Remove rind from grapefruit using a vegetable peeler, and discard bitter white pith. Cut the rind into julienne strips. Peel and section grapefruit.
2. Combine grapefruit rind, sections, and water in a large saucepan; bring to a boil. Reduce heat to medium, and simmer 15 minutes, stirring occasionally. Add cranberries, and cook 10 minutes. Add sugar; cook 30 minutes or until slightly thick, stirring occasionally. Pour into decorative jars or airtight containers. Store in refrigerator for up to 3 weeks. Yield: 5¼ cups (serving size: 2 tablespoons).

POINTS: 1; **Exchanges:** 1 Starch
Per serving: CAL 65 (0% from fat); PRO 0.2g; FAT 0g (sat 0g); CARB 16.8g; FIB 0.2g; CHOL 0mg; IRON 0mg; SOD 0mg; CALC 3mg

Sweet-and-Sour Dipping Sauce

1   cup mango chutney
2   tablespoons dark brown sugar
3   tablespoons Dijon mustard
2   tablespoons red wine vinegar
1   tablespoon vegetable oil
1   teaspoon hot sauce

1. Combine all ingredients in a bowl; stir well. Cover and chill. Serve with shrimp. Yield: 1½ cups (serving size: 1 tablespoon).

POINTS: 1; **Exchanges:** ½ Starch
Per serving: CAL 38 (17% from fat); PRO 0.1g; FAT 0.7g (sat 0.1g); CARB 7.9g; FIB 0g; CHOL 0mg; IRON 0.1mg; SOD 80mg; CALC 4mg

Grapefruit-Cranberry
Marmalade

Add additional herb sprigs to jars, if desired. Seal bottles with corks or airtight lids. Use in vinaigrettes, vegetable salads, soups, or stews. Yield: 3¾ cups (serving size: 1 tablespoon).

POINTS: 0; **Exchanges:** Free
Per serving: CAL 2 (0% from fat); PRO 0g; FAT 0g (sat 0g); CARB 0g; FIB 0g; CHOL 0mg; IRON 0mg; SOD 2mg; CALC 0mg

Spiced Vinegar

Whole nutmeg is the hard, 1-inch-long oval seed from the nutmeg tree and is available through higher end spice companies. Its flavor is superior to prepackaged ground nutmeg. Crack the hard, oval nutmeg with a hammer or nutcracker.

1 tablespoon whole cloves
1 tablespoon whole allspice
1 tablespoon black peppercorns
1 teaspoon cardamom seeds
1 (2-inch) cinnamon stick
1 whole nutmeg, cracked
4 cups red wine vinegar

1. Combine cloves, allspice, peppercorns, cardamom seeds, cinnamon stick, and nutmeg in a wide-mouth quart glass jar, and set aside. Bring vinegar to a boil in a nonaluminum saucepan. Pour hot vinegar over spices in jar; cover with metal lid and screw on band. Let stand at room temperature 2 weeks.

2. Pour mixture through a cheesecloth-lined fine sieve into decorative bottles or jars; discard spices. Seal bottles with corks or airtight lids. Use in vinaigrettes and in fruit or vegetable salads. Yield: 4 cups (serving size: 1 tablespoon).

POINTS: 0; **Exchanges:** Free
Per serving: CAL 3 (0% from fat); PRO 0g; FAT 0g (sat 0g); CARB 0.7g; FIB 0g; CHOL 0mg; IRON 0mg; SOD 0mg; CALC 0mg

Citrus Vinegar

10 (4-inch) strips orange rind
½   medium navel orange, peeled and sectioned
½   small grapefruit, peeled and sectioned
4   cups white wine vinegar

1. Combine first 3 ingredients in a wide-mouth quart glass jar; set aside.

2. Bring vinegar to a boil in a nonaluminum saucepan. Pour hot vinegar over fruit and rind in

Mixed Herb Vinegar, Spiced Vinegar, and Citrus Vinegar

Mixed Herb Vinegar

½   cup chopped fresh thyme
¼   cup chopped fresh parsley
¼   cup chopped fresh rosemary
¼   cup chopped fresh sage
4   green onions, thinly sliced
1   garlic clove, crushed
9   black peppercorns
3¾ cups white wine vinegar
Additional thyme, rosemary, or sage sprigs (optional)

1. Combine first 7 ingredients in a wide-mouth quart glass jar; set aside. Bring vinegar to a boil in a nonaluminum saucepan. Pour hot vinegar over herbs in jar; cover with metal lid and screw on band. Let stand at room temperature 2 weeks.

2. Pour mixture through a cheesecloth-lined fine sieve into decorative bottles or jars; discard herbs.

jar; cover with metal lid and screw on band. Let stand at room temperature 2 weeks.

3. Pour mixture through a cheesecloth-lined fine sieve into decorative bottles or jars; discard fruit and rind. Seal bottles with corks or airtight lids. Use in vinaigrettes and in fruit or vegetable salads. Yield: 4 cups (serving size: 1 tablespoon).

POINTS: 0; **Exchanges:** Free
Per serving: CAL 2 (0% from fat); PRO 0g; FAT 0g (sat 0g); CARB 0g; FIB 0g; CHOL 0mg; IRON 0mg; SOD 2mg; CALC 0mg

Hot Cider Punch

Whole spices add flavor without clouding the punch.

1   (2½-inch) cinnamon stick
5   whole cloves
10 whole allspice
8   cups apple cider
2   cups orange juice
¾   cup fresh lemon juice
¼   cup honey
1½ teaspoons butter or margarine

1. Wrap cinnamon stick, cloves, and allspice in a cheesecloth bag.

2. Combine spice bag, apple cider, and remaining ingredients in a large saucepan or Dutch oven; bring to a boil. Reduce heat, and simmer, uncovered, 1 hour. Discard spice bag. Yield: 8 cups (serving size: 1 cup).

POINTS: 4; **Exchanges:** 3 Fruit
Per serving: CAL 189 (5% from fat); PRO 0.7g; FAT 1g (sat 0.2g); CARB 46.4g; FIB 0.6g; CHOL 0mg; IRON 1mg; SOD 17mg; CALC 25mg

Citrus Marinade

You can use bottled juices to save time.

1   teaspoon grated orange rind
½   cup fresh orange juice
⅓   cup fresh grapefruit juice
1   teaspoon grated lime rind
2   tablespoons fresh lime juice
2   tablespoons vegetable oil
2   tablespoons honey
1   tablespoon white wine vinegar
1   teaspoon white wine Worcestershire sauce
½   teaspoon Dijon mustard
¼   teaspoon ground red pepper

1. Combine all ingredients in a medium bowl; stir well. Use immediately or store in refrigerator. Use to marinate chicken, pork, lamb, or fish. Yield: 1⅓ cups (serving size: 1 tablespoon).

POINTS: 1; **Exchanges:** ½ Fat
Per serving: CAL 20 (54% from fat); PRO 0.1g; FAT 1.2g (sat 0.2g); CARB 2.5g; FIB 0g; CHOL 0mg; IRON 0.1mg; SOD 5mg; CALC 1mg

Tartar Sauce

1   cup light mayonnaise
2   tablespoons sweet pickle relish
1   tablespoon chopped fresh parsley
1   tablespoon finely chopped onion
1   tablespoon chopped pimiento-stuffed olives

1. Combine all ingredients in a bowl; stir well. Cover and chill. Yield: 1¼ cups (serving size: 1 tablespoon).

POINTS: 1; **Exchanges:** 1 Fat
Per serving: CAL 38 (88% from fat); PRO 0.1g; FAT 3.7g (sat 0.6g); CARB 1.2g; FIB 0.1g; CHOL 5mg; IRON 0.1mg; SOD 87mg; CALC 2mg

Fast Rosemary-Raisin Focaccia

1   (1-pound) loaf frozen white bread dough, thawed
1   tablespoon dried rosemary
1   tablespoon raisins
Cooking spray
1   large egg white, lightly beaten

1. Turn dough out onto a lightly floured surface; knead in rosemary and raisins. Pat dough into a 9-inch circle on a large baking sheet coated with cooking spray. Cover and let rise in a warm place (85°), free from drafts, 15 minutes or until puffy.

2. Preheat oven to 400°.

3. Uncover dough. Using the handle of a wooden spoon or your fingertips, make indentations in top of dough. Gently brush dough with egg white. Bake at 400° for 20 minutes or until browned. Cut into wedges, and serve warm. Yield: 8 servings (serving size: 1 wedge).

POINTS: 3; **Exchanges:** 2 Starch
Per serving: CAL 157 (12% from fat); PRO 5.5g; FAT 2.1g (sat 0.5g); CARB 29.1g; FIB 0.1g; CHOL 1mg; IRON 0.3mg; SOD 287mg; CALC 46mg

VINEGAR VARIATIONS

Making your own flavored vinegar is as simple as pouring commercial vinegar over your favorite berries, herbs, or spices and storing the mixture for about 10 days. If you feel creative (or if you have an herb garden), use one of the herbed vinegar recipes on these pages and substitute the same amount of your favorite herb for the herb called for in the recipe.

The vinegar doesn't have to be heated when you pour it over the herbs, but when we made the vinegars in our kitchens, the final product was clearer when we used heated vinegar.

For flavor and color variations, pour cider, red wine, white wine, or champagne vinegar over the herbs.

Desserts

CURB YOUR CRAVING FOR SOMETHING SWEET
WITH THESE LOW-FAT TREATS.

Raspberry-Champagne Sorbet

Raspberry Angel Torte
looks impressive, but it's
a cinch to make.

Raspberry-Champagne Sorbet

1   cup water, divided
¾   cup sugar
2   cups raspberries
2   cups champagne, chilled

1. Combine ¾ cup water and sugar in a small saucepan; bring to a boil, stirring until sugar melts. Remove from heat; let cool completely.

2. Place remaining ¼ cup water and raspberries in a food processor; process until smooth. Strain mixture through a sieve into a bowl; discard seeds. Add sugar syrup and champagne to raspberry purée; stir well.

3. Pour mixture into the freezer can of an ice cream freezer; freeze according to manufacturer's instructions. Spoon sorbet into a freezer-safe container; cover and freeze 1 hour or until firm. Yield: 4 cups (serving size: ½ cup).

POINTS: 2; **Exchanges:** 1½ Starch
Per serving: CAL 132 (1% from fat); PRO 0.5g; FAT 0.2g (sat 0g); CARB 23g; FIB 2.3g; CHOL 0mg; IRON 0.5mg; SOD 3mg; CALC 9mg

Raspberry Angel Torte

2   cups raspberries
2   tablespoons sugar
2   tablespoons seedless raspberry jam, melted
1   (10-ounce) loaf angel food cake
6   tablespoons amaretto (almond-flavored liqueur), divided
¾   cup vanilla low-fat yogurt
½   cup blueberries
8   teaspoons sliced almonds, toasted

1. Place raspberries, sugar, and jam in a food processor, and pulse 3 times or until coarsely chopped. Set aside.

2. Line an 8-inch loaf pan with plastic wrap, allowing plastic wrap to extend over edge of pan. Cut cake horizontally into 6 slices (slices will be very thin). Place 1 cake slice in bottom of pan. Brush cake slice with 1 tablespoon amaretto. Spread 3 tablespoons raspberry mixture over cake slice; top with another cake slice. Repeat layers ending with cake slice (do not put amaretto or raspberry mixture on top cake layer). Cover and chill 2 hours.

3. Place a serving plate upside down on top of pan; invert cake onto plate. Remove plastic wrap. Combine yogurt and remaining 1 tablespoon amaretto in a small bowl; stir well. Cut torte crosswise into 8 slices. Dollop 1½ tablespoons yogurt mixture onto each slice; sprinkle each with 2 tablespoons blueberries and 1 teaspoon almonds. Yield: 8 servings.

POINTS: 4; **Exchanges:** 2½ Starch
Per serving: CAL 207 (7% from fat); PRO 4.1g; FAT 1.7g (sat 0.3g); CARB 39.7g; FIB 2.9g; CHOL 1mg; IRON 0.4mg; SOD 206mg; CALC 81mg

Easy Apricot Cake

1 cup sugar
5 tablespoons cornstarch
4 cups apricot nectar
1 (1½-pound) angel food cake, cut into 2-inch cubes (about 10 cups)
1 (8-ounce) container frozen reduced-calorie whipped topping, thawed
6 tablespoons flaked sweetened coconut, toasted

1. Combine sugar and cornstarch in a medium saucepan. Gradually add nectar, stirring until blended. Bring to a boil, and cook 1 minute or until thick and bubbly, stirring constantly. Spread half of apricot mixture in bottom of a 13- x 9-inch baking dish, and top with half of cake cubes. Repeat layers with remaining apricot mixture and cake cubes. Cover and chill 8 hours. Spread whipped topping evenly over cake cubes; sprinkle with toasted coconut. Yield: 10 servings (serving size: 1 cup).

POINTS: 5; **Exchanges:** 2 Starch, 1½ Fruit
Per serving: CAL 245 (10% from fat); PRO 3.3g; FAT 2.8g (sat 1.9g); CARB 53.1g; FIB 0.5g; CHOL 0mg; IRON 0.4mg; SOD 235mg; CALC 51mg

Berry Ambrosia With Mimosa Sauce

2 navel oranges, peeled and sectioned
1½ cups blueberries
1½ cups raspberries

1 tablespoon cornstarch
¾ cup orange juice
⅓ cup dry champagne
1 tablespoon light-colored corn syrup

1. Combine orange sections, blueberries, and raspberries in a bowl; toss gently. Cover and chill.
2. Combine cornstarch and orange juice in a small saucepan; stir well. Add champagne; bring to a boil, stirring constantly. Reduce heat, and simmer 1 minute, stirring constantly. Remove from heat; stir in corn syrup. Let cool to room temperature.
3. Spoon ½ cup fruit mixture into each of 8 individual dessert dishes. Spoon 2 tablespoons sauce over each serving. Yield: 8 servings.

POINTS: 0; **Exchanges:** 1 Fruit
Per serving: CAL 68 (4% from fat); PRO 0.9g; FAT 0.3g (sat 0g); CARB 16.8g; FIB 5g; CHOL 0mg; IRON 0.4mg; SOD 5mg; CALC 23mg

Pears Baked in Molasses-Port Sauce

6 Bosc pears, peeled, cored, and sliced
1 cup molasses
1 cup port or other sweet red wine
1 tablespoon butter or margarine, melted

1. Preheat oven to 350°.
2. Arrange pear slices in a 13- x 9-inch baking dish. Combine molasses, wine, and melted butter; drizzle over pears. Bake at 350° for 30 minutes or until tender, basting with molasses mixture every 10 minutes. Remove pear slices from dish; set aside, and keep warm. Pour molasses mixture into a small saucepan, and bring to a boil. Reduce heat, and simmer 30 minutes or until thick and syrupy, stirring occasionally.
3. Divide pear slices evenly among 6 dessert dishes; drizzle syrup evenly over pears. Serve warm. Yield: 6 servings.

POINTS: 5; **Exchanges:** 1 Fruit, 3 Starch
Per serving: CAL 274 (9% from fat); PRO 0.7g; FAT 2.6g (sat 0.4g); CARB 66.3g; FIB 4.3g; CHOL 5mg; IRON 3mg; SOD 43mg; CALC 131mg

Red Wine-and-Blueberry Granita

This grown-up dessert doesn't require any special equipment to make. Just freeze the mixture in a baking dish and then scrape with the tines of a fork until fluffy.

4   cups blueberries
Basic Sugar Syrup
2   cups dry red wine

1. Place blueberries in a food processor; process until smooth. Strain mixture through a sieve into a large saucepan; discard solids.

2. Add Basic Sugar Syrup and wine; bring mixture to a boil. Reduce heat, and simmer, uncovered, 3 minutes. Remove from heat, and let cool. Pour cooled mixture into an 8-inch square baking dish; cover and freeze at least 8 hours or until firm.

3. Remove mixture from freezer; scrape entire mixture with the tines of a fork until fluffy. Spoon into a container; cover and freeze for up to 1 month. Yield: 5 cups (serving size: ½ cup).

POINTS: 3; **Exchanges:** 1½ Starch, 1 Fruit
Per serving: CAL 179 (1% from fat); PRO 0.5g; FAT 0.2g (sat 0g); CARB 39.5g; FIB 2.7g; CHOL 0mg; IRON 0.3mg; SOD 7mg; CALC 7mg

Basic Sugar Syrup:

1½ cups sugar
1⅓ cups water

1. Combine sugar and water in a large saucepan, and stir well. Bring to a boil, and cook 1 minute or until sugar dissolves, stirring constantly. Yield: 2 cups.

Summer Fruit in Sparkling Cider

1   cup cubed fresh pineapple
1   cup sliced nectarines
¾   cup pitted fresh cherries
¾   cup seedless green grapes
½   cup sliced plums
1   cup sparkling apple cider, chilled

1. Combine first 5 ingredients in a medium glass bowl; toss gently. Cover and freeze 1 hour or until fruit mixture is partially frozen.

2. Pour cider over fruit mixture, and toss gently.

Serve immediately. Yield: 4 servings (serving size: about 1 cup).

POINTS: 2; **Exchanges:** 2 Fruit
Per serving: CAL 111 (7% from fat); PRO 1g; FAT 0.9g (sat 0.2g); CARB 27.1g; FIB 2.8g; CHOL 0mg; IRON 0.6mg; SOD 3mg; CALC 16mg

Chocolate Wafer Malts

8   cups vanilla fat-free frozen yogurt, softened and divided
2   cups 1% low-fat chocolate-flavored milk, divided
20 chocolate wafer cookies, coarsely crushed and divided

1. Combine 4 cups yogurt and 1 cup chocolate milk in a blender; process until smooth. Stir in half of crushed cookies, and pour into individual glasses. Repeat procedure with remaining yogurt, chocolate milk, and cookies. Serve immediately. Yield: 8 servings (serving size: 1 cup).

POINTS: 5; **Exchanges:** 3½ Starch
Per serving: CAL 260 (11% from fat); PRO 9.7g; FAT 3.3g (sat 1.1g); CARB 50.2g; FIB 0.1g; CHOL 12mg; IRON 0.4mg; SOD 208mg; CALC 345mg

Fruit and Crème Brûlée

Neufchâtel cheese is a soft, unripened cheese similar to cream cheese but with one-third the calories and fat. Block-style light cream cheese may be substituted.

2   cups cubed fresh pineapple
2   cups strawberries, halved
2   medium kiwifruit, peeled and sliced
¼   cup low-fat sour cream
2   ounces Neufchâtel cheese, softened (about ¼ cup)
⅓   cup firmly packed brown sugar

1. Combine first 3 ingredients in a bowl; stir gently. Divide evenly among 6 (6-ounce) ovenproof ramekins or custard cups.

2. Combine sour cream and cheese; stir well. Spoon evenly over fruit mixture. Place ramekins on a baking sheet. Sprinkle evenly with brown sugar. Broil 2 minutes or until sugar melts. Serve immediately. Yield: 6 servings.

POINTS: 2; **Exchanges:** 1 Fruit, ½ Starch, 1 Fat
Per serving: CAL 136 (26% from fat); PRO 2g; FAT 3.9g (sat 1.8g); CARB 24.8g; FIB 2.9g; CHOL 11mg; IRON 0.9mg; SOD 46mg; CALC 43mg

Red Wine-and-Blueberry Granita

Peach Melba Parfaits

4   cups vanilla low-fat ice cream, softened
1   cup peeled mashed peaches (about
     ¾ pound)
1   tablespoon amaretto (almond-flavored
     liqueur)
1   teaspoon vanilla extract
1   (12-ounce) package unsweetened frozen
     raspberries, thawed and undrained
3   tablespoons sugar
1   tablespoon Grand Marnier (orange-
     flavored liqueur)
1½   cups raspberries
8   peach slices (optional)

1. Combine first 4 ingredients in a freezer-safe container; stir well. Cover and freeze until firm.

2. Place thawed raspberries, sugar, and Grand Marnier in a blender; process until smooth. Strain mixture through a sieve into a bowl; discard seeds. Cover raspberry purée; chill.

3. Spoon 2 teaspoons raspberry purée into each of 8 parfait glasses or champagne flutes. Top each with about 1½ tablespoons raspberries and ¼ cup ice cream mixture. Repeat layers, ending with 2 teaspoons raspberry purée. Garnish with peach slices, if desired. Yield: 8 servings.

POINTS: 3; **Exchanges:** 1 Fruit, 1 Starch, ½ Fat
Per serving: CAL 165 (17% from fat); PRO 3.3g; FAT 3.2g (sat 1.8g); CARB 30.8g; FIB 5.2g; CHOL 9mg; IRON 0.5mg; SOD; 56mg; CALC 107mg

White Chocolate Bavarian Cream With Fresh Cherries

3   cups halved pitted sweet cherries (about
     1¼ pounds)
3   tablespoons kirsch (cherry brandy)
1½   cups skim milk
2   tablespoons sugar
1   large egg yolk, lightly beaten
1   envelope unflavored gelatin
3   ounces premium white chocolate, chopped
1¼   cups frozen reduced-calorie whipped
     topping, thawed
Mint leaves (optional)

1. Combine cherries and kirsch in a bowl; stir well. Cover and chill 30 minutes.

2. Combine milk, sugar, and egg yolk in a medium heavy-duty saucepan; stir well. Sprinkle gelatin over milk mixture; let stand 1 minute. Place over medium heat, and cook 12 minutes or until gelatin dissolves and mixture is slightly thick, stirring constantly with a whisk. Remove from heat; add white chocolate, stirring until chocolate melts and mixture is smooth. Pour white chocolate mixture into a medium bowl. Place bowl over a large ice-filled bowl, and let stand 15 minutes or just until mixture begins to thicken, stirring every 5 minutes (do not allow gelatin to set). Gently stir in whipped topping.

3. Spoon ¼ cup cherry mixture into each of 6

White Chocolate
Bavarian Cream With
Fresh Cherries

A MOUSSE OF DISTINCTION

Bavarian cream is a cold dessert mousse created from custard, whipped cream, gelatin, and flavorings such as chocolate and liqueurs. We lightened this version by substituting skim milk for whole milk and reduced-fat whipped topping for whipped cream. We also included cherries to boost the flavor. For this recipe and for eating out of hand, always choose sweet cherries, such as Bing; sour cherries, such as Montmorency, are good for making pies and preserves but are often too tart to eat raw.

   Here are a few tips for a smooth, creamy custard: Keep a watchful eye while heating the gelatin mixture so that it doesn't come to a boil. Remember to stir it constantly with a whisk. Also use a light hand while stirring the whipped topping into the white chocolate mixture.

(8-ounce) parfait glasses; top each with ¼ cup white chocolate mixture. Repeat layers with remaining cherry mixture and chocolate mixture. Cover and chill 1 hour. Garnish with mint leaves, if desired. Yield: 6 servings.

POINTS: 5; **Exchanges:** 2 Starch, 1½ Fat
Per serving: CAL 230 (30% from fat); PRO 5.7g; FAT 7.8g (sat 3g); CARB 33.7g; FIB 1.7g; CHOL 38mg; IRON 0.4mg; SOD 57mg; CALC 129mg

Orange Custard With Raspberry Dessert Sauce

¾ cup skim milk
3 tablespoons sugar
1 teaspoon grated orange rind
½ teaspoon vanilla extract
⅛ teaspoon salt
2 large egg yolks
Raspberry Dessert Sauce

1. Preheat oven to 350°.

2. Combine first 6 ingredients in a bowl; stir with a whisk until blended. Divide mixture evenly between 2 (6-ounce) custard cups. Place cups in a baking pan; add hot water to pan to a depth of 1 inch. Place in a 350° oven; immediately reduce oven temperature to 325°, and bake 1 hour and 10 minutes or until a knife inserted near center comes out clean. Remove cups from water; let cool. Cover and chill at least 4 hours.

3. Loosen edges of custard with a knife or a rubber spatula, and invert onto a serving plate. Serve with Raspberry Dessert Sauce. Yield: 2 servings (serving size: 1 custard and 2 tablespoons sauce).

POINTS: 4; **Exchanges:** 1 Fruit, 1½ Starch, ½ Hi-fat Meat
Per serving: CAL 221 (22% from fat); PRO 6.4g; FAT 5.5g (sat 1.7g); CARB 37.1g; FIB 3.3g; CHOL 220mg; IRON 1mg; SOD 203mg; CALC 146mg

Raspberry Dessert Sauce:

1 (10-ounce) package frozen raspberries in light syrup, thawed and undrained
2 tablespoons water
2 teaspoons cornstarch

1. Drain raspberries, reserving syrup. Press raspberries through a sieve, reserving purée; discard seeds. Combine water and cornstarch in a sauce-pan; stir until blended. Stir in reserved raspberry syrup and purée; bring to a boil, and cook 1 minute, stirring constantly. Pour into a bowl; let cool. Yield: ¾ cup (serving size: 2 tablespoons).

Note: Store remaining sauce in an airtight container in refrigerator up to 1 week. Serve over fruit, light ice cream, or angel food cake.

POINTS: 0; **Exchanges:** 1 Fruit
Per serving: CAL 52 (2% from fat); PRO 0.4g; FAT 0.1g (sat 0g); CARB 13.2g; FIB 3.3g; CHOL 0mg; IRON 0.3mg; SOD 0mg; CALC 7mg

Raspberry Cheesecake Parfaits

Raspberry jam melts in just a few seconds in the microwave.

¼ cup light ricotta cheese
¼ cup block-style fat-free cream cheese
2 tablespoons sugar
1 cup raspberries
2 tablespoons seedless raspberry jam, melted
6 tablespoons vanilla wafer cookie crumbs (about 10 cookies)
2 tablespoons frozen reduced-calorie whipped topping, thawed

1. Place first 3 ingredients in a food processor; process until smooth, scraping sides of processor bowl once.

2. Combine raspberries and melted raspberry spread; stir gently. Spoon ¼ cup raspberry mixture into each of 2 (8-ounce) parfait glasses. Top each with 2 tablespoons cheese mixture, 3 tablespoons cookie crumbs, 2 tablespoons cheese mixture, ¼ cup raspberry mixture, and 1 tablespoon whipped topping. Chill at least 2 hours before serving. Yield: 2 servings.

POINTS: 4; **Exchanges:** 2½ Starch, 1 Fat
Per serving: CAL 244 (22% from fat); PRO 8.6g; FAT 5.9g (sat 2.1g); CARB 40.2g; FIB 4.6g; CHOL 9mg; IRON 0.7mg; SOD 269mg; CALC 138mg

Tangerine Tapioca

2½ cups 2% reduced-fat milk
2½ teaspoons grated orange rind
⅓ cup sugar
3 tablespoons uncooked quick-cooking tapioca
1 large egg, lightly beaten

½ cup tangerine juice
6 orange sections (optional)

1. Combine milk and orange rind in a 2-quart glass measure. Microwave at HIGH 5 minutes or until milk is 180° and tiny bubbles form around edge (do not boil). Add sugar, tapioca, and egg to milk mixture; stir well. Microwave at HIGH 5 minutes or until slightly thick. Let stand 5 minutes. Stir in juice.

2. Press plastic wrap onto surface of pudding, and chill. Spoon pudding into individual dessert dishes, and garnish with orange sections, if desired. Yield: 4 servings (serving size: ¾ cup).

POINTS: 4; **Exchanges:** 1½ Starch, ½ L-F Milk
Per serving: CAL 197 (19% from fat); PRO 6.8g; FAT 4.2g (sat 2.2g); CARB 33.5g; FIB 0g; CHOL 65mg; IRON 0.4mg; SOD 93mg; CALC 201mg

Devil's Food Cookies

¼ cup stick margarine, softened
⅔ cup sugar
½ cup low-fat buttermilk
1 teaspoon vanilla extract
2 egg whites
1½ cups all-purpose flour
½ cup unsweetened cocoa
1 teaspoon baking soda
¼ teaspoon salt
Cooking spray
2 teaspoons sifted powdered sugar

1. Preheat oven to 350°.

2. Cream margarine; add ⅔ cup sugar, and beat at medium speed of a mixer until blended. Add buttermilk, vanilla, and egg whites; beat well. Combine flour, cocoa, baking soda, and salt; add to creamed mixture, mixing well.

3. Drop dough by tablespoonfuls 2 inches apart onto cookie sheets coated with cooking spray. Bake at 350° for 7 minutes. Remove from pan; cool completely on wire racks. Sprinkle with powdered sugar. Yield: 2½ dozen (serving size: 1 cookie).

POINTS: 1; **Exchanges:** ½ Starch, ½ Fat
Per serving: CAL 64 (26% from fat); PRO 1.5g; FAT 1.8g (sat 0.4g); CARB 10.4g; FIB 0.2g; CHOL 0mg; IRON 0.5mg; SOD 73mg; CALC 15mg

You're in for a dark, chocolaty, sinfully delicious treat with Devil's Food Cookies.

3. Combine milk, lime rind, lime juice, and egg yolks in a large bowl; beat at low speed of a mixer until smooth. Add flour mixture; beat well.

4. Beat egg whites at high speed of a mixer until stiff peaks form. Gently fold egg whites into lime mixture.

5. Spoon mixture into a 1-quart soufflé dish. Place dish in an 8-inch square baking pan, and add hot water to pan to a depth of 1 inch. Bake at 350° for 45 minutes or until top of soufflé looks set like a cake and springs back when lightly touched in center (bottom of soufflé will be saucy).

6. Remove dish from water. Divide cake-like top evenly among 6 dessert dishes; spoon saucy mixture from bottom of dish evenly over each serving. Yield: 6 servings.

POINTS: 3; **Exchanges:** 1½ Starch
Per serving: CAL 123 (12% from fat); PRO 4.7g; FAT 1.7g (sat 0.6g); CARB 22.9g; FIB 0.1g; CHOL 67mg; IRON 0.5mg; SOD 150mg; CALC 46mg

Foolproof Apple Cake

Be sure to spoon flour into a dry measuring cup; then level the flour with a straight edge. Too much flour will make the cake dry.

2   cups peeled chopped Granny Smith apple
¾   cup sugar
1½ cups all-purpose flour
1   teaspoon baking soda
1   teaspoon baking powder
1   teaspoon ground cinnamon
½   teaspoon salt
¼   cup vegetable oil
½   teaspoon vanilla extract
1   large egg white, lightly beaten
Cooking spray

1. Preheat oven to 350°.

2. Combine apple and sugar in a bowl; stir well. Let stand 10 minutes.

3. Combine flour and next 4 ingredients in a large bowl; make a well in center of mixture. Combine apple mixture, oil, vanilla, and egg white. Add to dry ingredients, stirring well (batter will resemble streusel topping).

4. Press batter gently into an 8-inch square baking

End an Italian meal with the unusual yet simple flavors of Strawberries With Balsamic Vinegar.

Strawberries With Balsamic Vinegar

4   cups strawberries, halved
1   tablespoon sugar
1   tablespoon balsamic vinegar

1. Combine all ingredients in a bowl; toss well. Let stand 30 minutes. Toss well before serving. Yield: 4 servings (serving size: 1 cup).

POINTS: 0; **Exchanges:** 1 Fruit
Per serving: CAL 57 (9% from fat); PRO 0.9g; FAT 0.6g (sat 0g); CARB 13.6g; FIB 3.9g; CHOL 0mg; IRON 0.6mg; SOD 2mg; CALC 21mg

Baked Lime Soufflé

½   cup sugar
¼   cup all-purpose flour
¼   teaspoon salt
⅔   cup skim milk
1½ teaspoons grated lime rind
¼   cup lime juice
2   large egg yolks
4   large egg whites (at room temperature)

1. Preheat oven to 350°.

2. Combine first 3 ingredients in a small bowl; stir well, and set aside.

pan coated with cooking spray. Bake at 350° for 30 minutes or until a wooden pick inserted in center comes out clean. Let cool completely in pan on a wire rack. Yield: 9 servings.

POINTS: 4; **Exchanges:** 1½ Starch, 1 Fruit, 1 Fat
Per serving: CAL 206 (28% from fat); PRO 2.4g; FAT 6.4g (sat 1.1g); CARB 35.4g; FIB 1.2g; CHOL 0mg; IRON 1mg; SOD 262mg; CALC 49mg

Strawberry-Apricot Caramel Sundaes

Available mainly in June and July, fresh apricots are highly perishable and should be refrigerated in a plastic bag for no more than 3 to 5 days before eating.

1   cup chopped apricots (about 6 ounces)
1   cup sliced strawberries
2   tablespoons orange juice
2   cups vanilla low-fat ice cream
¼   cup fat-free butterscotch-flavored sundae syrup
4   teaspoons chopped pistachios
Sugar cookies (optional)

1. Combine first 3 ingredients in a bowl; stir well. Cover and chill 30 minutes. Spoon ice cream into stemmed glasses; top with fruit mixture and syrup. Sprinkle with pistachios. Serve with sugar cookies, if desired. Yield: 4 servings (serving size: ½ cup ice cream, ½ cup fruit, 1 tablespoon syrup, and 1 teaspoon pistachios).

POINTS: 5; **Exchanges:** 1 Fruit, 1½ Starch, 1 Fat
Per serving: CAL 229 (28% from fat); PRO 5g; FAT 7.2g (sat 2.3g); CARB 38.4g; FIB 2.7g; CHOL 9mg; IRON 1mg; SOD 93mg; CALC 115mg

Blueberry Crumble Pie

5   cups fresh or frozen blueberries
1   (9-inch) reduced-fat graham cracker crust
¾   cup firmly packed brown sugar
3   tablespoons all-purpose flour
1½ teaspoons vanilla extract
¼   teaspoon grated lemon rind
1   (8-ounce) carton low-fat sour cream
¼   cup dry breadcrumbs
1   tablespoon granulated sugar
1   tablespoon margarine, melted

1. Preheat oven to 375°.

2. Place blueberries in crust. Combine brown

sugar and next 4 ingredients in a bowl; stir well. Spread mixture over blueberries.

3. Combine breadcrumbs, granulated sugar, and margarine in a small bowl; stir well. Sprinkle over sour cream mixture. Bake at 375° for 40 minutes or until set and crumbs are lightly browned. Let cool 1 hour on a wire rack. Yield: 8 servings (serving size: 1 slice).

POINTS: 6; **Exchanges:** 1 Fruit, 2½ Starch, 1 Fat
Per serving: CAL 312 (24% from fat); PRO 3.2g; FAT 8.4g (sat 2.5g); CARB 56.5g; FIB 4.3g; CHOL 11mg; IRON 1.3mg; SOD 166mg; CALC 61mg

Double-Chocolate Satin Pudding

⅓   cup sugar
2   tablespoons cornstarch
2   tablespoons unsweetened cocoa
1   teaspoon instant espresso or 2 teaspoons instant coffee granules
⅛   teaspoon salt
1¾ cups 2% reduced-fat milk
1   (1-ounce) square semisweet chocolate, chopped
1   teaspoon vanilla extract

1. Combine first 5 ingredients in a medium saucepan, and stir well. Gradually add milk, stirring with a whisk. Bring to a boil over medium

Strawberry-Apricot Caramel Sundaes are a fruit-filled summer treat. Serve them with wafer cookies.

Peaches-and-Cream
Ice Cream

heat, stirring constantly. Add chocolate; cook 1 minute, stirring constantly. Remove from heat; stir in vanilla. Pour into a medium bowl; cover surface of pudding with heavy-duty plastic wrap, and chill at least 2 hours. Yield: 4 servings (serving size: ½ cup).

POINTS: 4; **Exchanges**: 2 Starch, ½ Fat
Per serving: CAL 182 (23% from fat); PRO 4.8g; FAT 4.6g (sat 3g); CARB 31.2g; FIB 0.2g; CHOL 8mg; IRON 0.8mg; SOD 126mg; CALC 138mg

Chocolate Chip Bars

6 tablespoons margarine, softened
⅓ cup sugar
¾ cup firmly packed dark brown sugar
2 large egg whites
2 teaspoons vanilla extract
2½ cups all-purpose flour
½ teaspoon baking soda
⅛ teaspoon salt
½ cup semisweet chocolate minichips
Cooking spray

1. Preheat oven to 375°.

2. Cream margarine and sugars at medium speed of a mixer until light and fluffy. Add egg whites and vanilla; beat well.

3. Combine flour, baking soda, and salt in a medium bowl; gradually add to creamed mixture, beating well. Stir in chocolate minichips.

4. Press cookie dough into bottom of a 13- x 9-inch baking pan coated with cooking spray. Bake at 375° for 10 minutes. Let cool in pan. Yield: 4 dozen (serving size: 1 bar).

POINTS: 1; **Exchanges**: ½ Starch, ½ Fat
Per serving: CAL 67 (30% from fat); PRO 0.9g; FAT 2.2g (sat 0.7g); CARB 11g; FIB 0.2g; CHOL 0mg; IRON 0.4mg; SOD 35mg; CALC 7mg

Russian Blueberry-Raspberry Pudding

2 cups blueberries
2 cups raspberries
1 cup plain low-fat yogurt
¼ cup firmly packed brown sugar

1. Divide berries evenly among 4 (8-ounce) ramekins or custard cups. Spoon ¼ cup yogurt over each serving; sprinkle evenly with sugar. Place ramekins on a baking sheet. Broil 3 minutes or until sugar melts. Serve immediately. Yield: 4 servings.

POINTS: 2; **Exchanges**: 1 Fruit, 1 Starch
Per serving: CAL 150 (10% from fat); PRO 3.7g; FAT 1.6g (sat 0g); CARB 32.1g; FIB 7.9g; CHOL 0mg; IRON 0.6mg; SOD 44mg; CALC 113mg

Peaches-and-Cream Ice Cream

5 cups 1% low-fat milk, divided
4 large egg yolks
2 (14-ounce) cans fat-free sweetened condensed skim milk
4 cups peeled mashed ripe peaches (about 8 medium)
2 tablespoons fresh lemon juice
2 tablespoons vanilla extract
½ teaspoon ground ginger
½ teaspoon almond extract
Mint sprigs (optional)

1. Combine 2½ cups 1% low-fat milk and egg yolks in a heavy saucepan; stir well with a whisk. Place over medium heat, and cook 10 minutes or until mixture is thick and coats a spoon, stirring constantly (do not boil). Combine egg yolk mixture, remaining 2½ cups 1% low-fat milk, condensed skim milk, peaches, and next 4 ingredients in a large bowl; stir well. Cover and chill.

2. Pour mixture into the freezer can of an ice cream freezer; freeze according to manufacturer's instructions. Spoon ice cream into a freezer-safe container; cover and freeze 1 hour or until firm. Garnish with mint sprigs, if desired. Yield: 24 servings (serving size: ½ cup).

POINTS: 3; **Exchanges**: 1½ Starch
Per serving: CAL 140 (9% from fat); PRO 4.9g; FAT 1.4g (sat 0.6g); CARB 26.2g; FIB 0.5g; CHOL 40mg; IRON 0.2mg; SOD 60mg; CALC 135mg

Rum-Mango Frozen Yogurt

2 cups peeled cubed mango
¼ cup sugar
¼ cup white rum
4 cups vanilla fat-free frozen yogurt, softened
Cooking spray

1. Combine cubed mango, sugar, and white rum in a medium bowl; stir well. Cover and chill 2 hours.

2. Place frozen mango mixture in a food processor; process until smooth, scraping sides of bowl once. Stir in yogurt. Spoon into a 6-cup mold coated with cooking spray; cover and freeze until firm. Unmold onto a serving plate. Serve immediately. Yield: 6 servings.

POINTS: 4; **Exchanges:** 2½ Starch, ½ Fruit
Per serving: CAL 218 (0% from fat); PRO 5.6g; FAT 0.1g (sat 0g); CARB 45.7g; FIB 0.8g; CHOL 0mg; IRON 0.1mg; SOD 95mg; CALC 205mg

Brown Sugar Icebox Cookies

1   cup all-purpose flour
¼   teaspoon baking soda
⅛   teaspoon salt
4   tablespoons stick margarine, softened
⅔   cup firmly packed brown sugar
1   teaspoon vanilla extract
1   large egg white
Cooking spray

1. Combine first 3 ingredients in a bowl; stir well, and set aside. Beat margarine at medium speed of a mixer until light and fluffy. Gradually add sugar, beating at medium speed of a mixer until well blended. Add vanilla and egg white; beat well. Add flour mixture, stirring until well blended. Turn dough out onto wax paper; shape into a 6-inch log. Wrap log in wax paper; freeze 3 hours or until very firm.

2. Preheat oven to 350°.

3. Cut log into 24 (¼-inch) slices, and place slices 1 inch apart on a baking sheet coated with cooking spray. Bake at 350° for 8 minutes. Remove from pans; let cool on wire racks. Yield: 2 dozen (serving size: 1 cookie).

POINTS: 1; **Exchanges:** ½ Starch, ½ Fat
Per serving: CAL 60 (30% from fat); PRO 0.7g; FAT 2g (sat 0.4g); CARB 10g; FIB 0.1g; CHOL 0mg; IRON 0.4mg; SOD 52mg; CALC 7mg

Spice Variation: Add ½ teaspoon ground cinnamon and ⅛ teaspoon ground cloves to flour mixture.

Freckled Chocolate Variation: Add 1 ounce grated semisweet chocolate to flour mixture.

Espresso Mocha Variation: Add 2 teaspoons instant espresso granules or 4 teaspoons instant coffee granules to flour mixture.

Butterscotch Bars

3   tablespoons stick margarine
½   cup firmly packed brown sugar
2   cups miniature marshmallows
4   cups oven-roasted rice cereal (such as Rice Krispies)
2   cups whole-wheat flake cereal (such as Wheaties)
Cooking spray

1. Melt margarine in a large saucepan over medium heat. Add sugar; stir well. Add marshmallows; cook until marshmallows melt, stirring constantly. Remove from heat; stir in cereals.

2. Press cereal mixture evenly into the bottom of a 13- x 9-inch baking pan coated with cooking spray. Let cool at least 1 hour; cut into squares. Yield: 18 servings.

POINTS: 2; **Exchanges:** 1 Starch, ½ Fat
Per serving: CAL 92 (20% from fat); PRO 0.8g; FAT 2g (sat 0.4g); CARB 18g; FIB 0.3g; CHOL 0mg; IRON 0.9mg; SOD 111mg; CALC 13mg

Nectarines With Port

1   cup ruby port or other sweet red wine
2   tablespoons sugar
1   (3-inch) cinnamon stick
6   medium nectarines (about 1½ pounds), each cut into 16 wedges
Mint sprigs (optional)

1. Combine first 3 ingredients in a saucepan; stir well. Place over medium-high heat, and cook 10 minutes or until reduced to 6 tablespoons. Remove from heat; discard cinnamon stick. Spoon 1 tablespoon wine mixture into each of 6 dessert dishes; top with 16 nectarine wedges. Garnish with mint, if desired. Yield: 6 servings.

POINTS: 1; **Exchanges:** 1 Fruit
Per serving: CAL 74 (7% from fat); PRO 1g; FAT 0.6g (sat 0.1g); CARB 18.1g; FIB 2.5g; CHOL 0mg; IRON 0.4mg; SOD 3mg; CALC 9mg

Chocolate Angel Food Cakes

½   cup plus 1 tablespoon sifted cake flour
⅓   cup sugar
2   tablespoons unsweetened cocoa
6   large egg whites
¾   teaspoon cream of tartar
Dash of salt
¼   cup sugar
½   teaspoon vanilla extract
¼   teaspoon almond extract
Cooking spray
1½ teaspoons powdered sugar
Raspberries (optional)

1. Preheat oven to 350°.

2. Sift together first 3 ingredients. Repeat procedure 3 times; set aside.

3. Beat egg whites, cream of tartar, and salt at high speed of a mixer until foamy. Gradually add ¼ cup sugar, beating until soft peaks form. Sift flour mixture over egg white mixture, ¼ cup at a time; fold in flour after each addition. Fold in extracts.

4. Spoon batter evenly into 4 (4-inch) tube pans heavily coated with cooking spray, spreading evenly. Bake at 350° for 25 minutes or until cakes spring back when lightly touched. Invert pans; let cakes cool upside down in pans 40 minutes. Loosen cakes from sides of pans using a narrow metal knife. Invert cakes onto individual plates. Sift powdered sugar over cooled cakes. Garnish with raspberries, if desired. Yield: 4 servings.

Note: You can order a mini angel food pan with 4 (4-inch) tube pan-shaped depressions from Wilton Industries. To order, call the company at 1-800-794-5866. Cost is $14.99, plus shipping and handling.

POINTS: 4; **Exchanges:** 3 Starch
Per serving: CAL 222 (3% from fat); PRO 7.1g; FAT 0.7g (sat 0.2g); CARB 46.5g; FIB 0.5g; CHOL 0mg; IRON 1.5mg; SOD 116mg; CALC 10mg

Peanut Butter Balls

1½ cups vanilla wafer crumbs
1   cup sifted powdered sugar
2   tablespoons unsweetened cocoa

Choose your favorite in-season berry to serve with Chocolate Angel Food Cakes.

Pistachio-Pineapple Pudding

½ cup plus 1 tablespoon light-colored corn
   syrup
6 tablespoons creamy peanut butter
2 tablespoons sifted powdered sugar

1. Combine first 3 ingredients; stir well. Combine corn syrup and peanut butter; stir well. Add peanut butter mixture to crumb mixture; stir well. Shape into 1-inch balls. Sprinkle 2 tablespoons powdered sugar evenly over balls. Store in an airtight container. Yield: 44 candies (serving size: 1 candy).

POINTS: 1; **Exchanges:** ½ Starch, ½ Fat
Per serving: CAL 53 (31% from fat); PRO 0.8g; FAT 1.8g (sat 0.2g); CARB 8.5g; FIB 0.1g; CHOL 0mg; IRON 0.1mg; SOD 28mg; CALC 28mg

Pistachio-Pineapple Pudding

1 (1-ounce) package sugar-free pistachio
   instant pudding mix
1 (8-ounce) carton plain low-fat yogurt
1 (8-ounce) carton vanilla low-fat yogurt
1 (8-ounce) can unsweetened crushed
   pineapple, drained
1 cup plus 6 tablespoons frozen reduced-
   calorie whipped topping, thawed and
   divided

1. Combine first 4 ingredients in a bowl; stir well. Fold in 1 cup whipped topping. Cover and chill. Spoon ½ cup pudding into each of 6 individual bowls, and top each serving with 1 tablespoon whipped topping. Yield: 6 servings.

POINTS: 2; **Exchanges:** 1 Starch, ½ Fat
Per serving: CAL 106 (25% from fat); PRO 4.6g; FAT 3g (sat 2g); CARB 15.7g; FIB 0.2g; CHOL 4mg; IRON 0.1mg; SOD 65mg; CALC 153mg

Chocolate-Cinnamon Fondue

Serve fondue with strawberries, banana chunks, orange sections, and cubed low-fat pound cake.

4 tablespoons stick margarine
8 ounces bittersweet chocolate, coarsely
   chopped
¼ cup all-purpose flour
2 cups light-colored corn syrup
¼ cup Kahlúa (coffee-flavored liqueur)
½ teaspoon ground cinnamon

1. Melt margarine and chocolate in a small saucepan over medium heat, stirring frequently. Add flour, stirring with a whisk until blended. Cook 1 minute, stirring constantly. Add corn syrup and Kahlúa; cook 1 minute. Remove from heat; stir in cinnamon. Pour into a fondue pot, and keep warm. Yield: 3 cups (serving size: 1 tablespoon).

Note: If fondue is not served immediately, pour into a bowl, and press heavy-duty plastic wrap onto surface of fondue. Pour into fondue pot to warm.

POINTS: 2; **Exchanges:** ½ Starch, ½ Fat
Per serving: CAL 77 (28% from fat); PRO 0.3g; FAT 2.4g (sat 1g); CARB 13.9g; FIB 0g; CHOL 0mg; IRON 0.2mg; SOD 28mg; CALC 2mg

Lemon Cookies

2½ cups sifted cake flour
¾ cup sugar
2 teaspoons baking powder
¼ teaspoon salt
6 tablespoons chilled stick margarine,
   cut into small pieces
2 tablespoons grated lemon rind
1 tablespoon lemon juice
1 large egg, lightly beaten
Cooking spray
2 tablespoons powdered sugar

1. Preheat oven to 350°.

2. Place cake flour, ¾ cup sugar, baking powder, and salt in a food processor; pulse 2 times or until blended. Add margarine and lemon rind; process until mixture resembles coarse meal. Add lemon juice and egg; process until dough leaves sides of bowl and forms a ball. Gently press mixture into a ball; wrap in heavy-duty plastic wrap, and chill 1 hour.

3. Shape dough into 42 (1-inch) balls; place 2 inches apart on baking sheets coated with cooking spray. Bake at 350° for 12 minutes. Remove cookies from pan, and roll in powdered sugar. Let cool completely on wire racks. Yield: 3½ dozen (serving size: 1 cookie).

POINTS: 2; **Exchanges:** 1 Starch, ½ Fat
Per serving: CAL 92 (30% from fat); PRO 1.1g; FAT 3.1g (sat 0.6g); CARB 14.9g; FIB 0g; CHOL 9mg; IRON 0.8mg; SOD 61mg; CALC 19mg

allspice A pea-size berry from the pimiento tree, named because it tastes like a combination of cloves, cinnamon, and nutmeg. Purchased as whole berries or ground, it is used in both savory and sweet dishes.

amaretto An almond-flavored liqueur originally from Italy.

balsamic vinegar An Italian vinegar made from white Trebbiano grapes. Aged over a period of years in wooden barrels, the vinegar has a dark color and pungent sweetness.

bulgur A nutritious food popular in the Middle East. It is made of wheat kernels that have been steamed, dried, and crushed. Bulgur is often confused with cracked wheat.

cake flour A soft-wheat flour with a fine texture and high starch content used to produce very tender cakes and pastries.

caper A flower bud from a Mediterranean bush. The buds are picked, sun-dried, and pickled in a salty vinegar brine.

cilantro The fresh leaves from the coriander plant. Widely used in Asian and Latin American cooking, it has a pungent flavor that lends itself to spicy foods.

couscous A staple of North African dining made from semolina, a coarsely ground durum wheat used to make pasta. It takes just 5 minutes to prepare and can be used much like rice.

currants Dried seedless Zante grapes, resembling tiny raisins.

curry powder A traditional Indian blend of up to 20 herbs, spices, and seeds. It is available in two degrees of spiciness: standard and hot (Madras).

Feta cheese A white and crumbly Greek cheese with a rich, tangy flavor. Traditionally made with sheep's or goat's milk.

fontina cheese A mild, semifirm Italian cheese that melts easily and smoothly.

ginger A common spice known for its peppery and sweet flavor. Ginger comes in several forms: fresh (the gnarled root), dried ground, crystallized, and pickled.

julienne To cut into thin matchlike strips, especially vegetables.

kiwifruit An oblong fruit that has a rough brown covering on the outside and bright-green flesh flecked with tiny edible black seeds. Eaten peeled, the fruit tastes similar to pineapple and strawberry.

kumquat The smallest member of the citrus family, cultivated in China, Japan, and the United States. The whole fruit, including the skin, is edible.

leek Similar in appearance to a giant scallion with a cylindrical white bulb and dark-green leaves. The flavor is like those of garlic and onion but milder and more subtle.

mango A golden-fleshed, juicy, and exotically sweet fruit. The flesh must be carefully carved away from the huge flat seed that traverses the length of the fruit.

molasses The brownish-black syrup produced during the refining of sugar cane and sugar beets.

paprika A common seasoning made from aromatic sweet red pepper pods. The flavor ranges from mild to hot.

polenta A northern Italian staple made from cooking cornmeal with milk or water until thick.

port wine A wine to which grape alcohol is added to stop the fermentation process, leaving the wine with plenty of sweetness.

portobello mushroom A large brown mushroom with a meaty, dense texture.

ramekin A baking dish, usually made of porcelain or earthenware, that resembles a miniature soufflé dish.

saffron The world's most expensive spice, made from the yellow-orange stigma of a purple crocus. Each stigma must be carefully hand-picked and dried. Luckily, saffron is flavorful, so a little goes a long way.

shallot A plant related to the onion but formed with a divided bulb like garlic. The shallot has a mild onion flavor.

shiitake mushroom A mushroom with a full-bodied, meaty flavor. The tough stem should be removed.

watercress A plant that grows in cool, running streams and whose pungent, peppery-tasting leaves are often used in salads and soups and as a garnish. Part of the mustard family.

Nutrition and Serving-Size Information

Here are some specific guidelines *Weight Watchers* Magazine adheres to regarding our recipes. For nutritional accuracy, please follow our suggestions.

• When preparing a recipe that yields more than one serving, it is important to mix the ingredients well and then divide the mixture evenly.

• Where liquid and solid parts have to be divided evenly, drain the liquid and set it aside. Evenly divide the remaining ingredients; then add equal amounts of the liquid to each serving.

• Unless otherwise indicated, selections of meat, poultry, and fish refer to cooked, skinned, and boned servings.

• The selection information is designated as follows: P/M (Protein/Milk), FA (Fat), FR/V (Fruit/Vegetable), B (Bread), C (Bonus Calories).

• The selection information no longer contains fractions: B, FR/V, and FA are rounded up if 0.5 or above; P/M is rounded up if 0.75 or above; and C only includes bonus calories above 30. If all of the selections are rounded up, bonus calories are decreased; if all of the selections are rounded down, bonus calories are increased.

• Recipes also provide approximate nutritional data, including the following: cal (calories), pro (protein), fat (total fat), sat (saturated fat), carb (carbohydrates), fib (dietary fiber), chol (cholesterol), iron (iron), sod (sodium), calc (calcium). Measurements are abbreviated as follows: g (grams), mg (milligrams).

Note: Because data on fat distribution are not available for some processed foods, these breakdowns should be considered approximate.

• Recipes include *POINTS*™ based on Weight Watchers International's 1•2•3 Success™ Weight Loss Plan. (Please turn to page 3 for more information about this plan.)

• *POINTS* are calculated from a formula based on calories, fat, and fiber that assigns higher points to higher-calorie, higher-fat foods. Based on your present weight, you are allowed a certain amount of *POINTS* per day.

• The recipes that are shown in our photographs may vary as to the number of servings pictured. It is important that you refer to the recipes for the exact serving information.

U S E F U L   E Q U I V A L E N T S
F O R   L I Q U I D   I N G R E D I E N T S   B Y   V O L U M E

	Fahrenheit	Celsius	Gas Mark
Freeze Water	32° F	0°C	
Room Temperature	68° F	20° C	
Boil Water	212° F	100° C	
Bake	325° F	160° C	3
	350° F	180° C	4
	375° F	190° C	5
	400° F	200° C	6
	425° F	220° C	7
	450° F	230° C	8
Broil			Grill